THERE
AND BACK AGAIN

THERE
AND BACK AGAIN

LESSONS FOR THE SHORT-TERM MISSIONARY

LEE DAVIS

ANEKO
PRESS

We enjoy hearing from our readers. Please contact us at www.anekopress.com/questions-comments with any questions, comments, or suggestions.

Cover Designer: J. Martin

Editor: Paul Miller

Aneko Press

www.anekopress.com

Aneko Press, Life Sentence Publishing, and our logos are trademarks of

Life Sentence Publishing, Inc.
203 E. Birch Street
P.O. Box 652
Abbotsford, WI 54405

RELIGION / Christian Ministry / Missions

Paperback ISBN: 979-8-88936-466-5

eBook ISBN: 979-8-88936-467-2

10   9   8   7   6   5   4   3   2   1

Available where books are sold

Contents

Part Three

Introduction

One of the greatest factors in my spiritual growth has been my involvement in missions, both stateside and overseas. I have been blessed to have been able to serve God on short-term mission trips in ten different states and ten different countries. The purpose of this book is to help prepare others who are also feeling called to serve God on a short-term mission trip.

My first foreign mission trip was to the mountains of Brazil just north of Rio. I was seventeen years old. I remember being surrounded by people, but I felt completely isolated and alone. The only people I was able to communicate with were other team members and our translator. It had only been a few months since I had responded to God's call on my life and had surrendered to the ministry. I wondered, *What am I doing here? Did I make the right choice?*

Here I was in a different country, thousands of miles away from home, surrounded by people I did not know, trying to communicate in a language I could not speak, eating food I did not like, and missing conveniences and comforts – and there was nothing I could do about it. I look back on that first experience and wish that someone would have warned me. Why are there so few resources to prepare everyday Christians as they step out in faith to help do their part in fulfilling the Great Commission? That is why I wrote this book – to help prepare others physically, emotionally, and spiritually for their missionary journey.

Anytime you begin something new, there is always a period of growing pains as you acquire new skills, adapt to new challenges, and learn difficult lessons. My hope is that you will be able to glean valuable lessons from my experiences, both good and bad. One of the first lessons I learned was *flexibility*, and that will be important for you to have as you read through this book. You will need to read this book with an open heart and mind. It does not matter if we are talking about team unity, prayer, attitudes, or external challenges; if you are unable to be flexible, then you will struggle. God is fully aware of every situation and is in complete control of our circumstances. We need to trust that He has orchestrated everything for our good and His glory, just as His Word tells us.

There is a famous scene from the television show *Friends* in which Ross, Rachel, and Chandler are carrying a couch up the stairs. Ross has drawn a diagram detailing exactly what they need to do for them to be successful. It isn't very long before his plan is failing, and in order to keep the couch from getting stuck as they navigate the winding staircase, Ross keeps yelling, "Pivot!" It has come to be a very funny and memorable moment, but when we find ourselves in situations that do not match our game plan, we do not find ourselves laughing. Do not panic. If you encounter something on your mission trip that you were not expecting, then fall to your knees, pray, and *pivot*. You are not encountering anything that God did not see coming.

My prayer for you is that you will be encouraged and blessed by these devotionals and that the lessons I have learned will be helpful to you as you prepare to serve God wherever He may be calling you.

How to Use this Book

This book is divided into three parts. Part One consists of stories and lessons that I have learned during the past thirty years of short-term mission work. It addresses the importance of team dynamics, spiritual warfare, physical and emotional challenges, kingdom purpose, and more.

Part Two is a thirty-day devotional that will guide you through the Bible prior to your mission trip. It will help to prepare you spiritually for obstacles you may encounter and to encourage you to rely on the leading of the Holy Spirit. Many of the devotionals in Part Two were written by my uncle, Malcolm Cheek, who played a huge role in helping me develop a heart for short-term mission work.

Part Three is a thirty-day devotional that you will begin after you return home. It is designed to help you recognize and manage the many emotions you will face as you strive to reacclimate to life at home. There may be pressure to conform, as well as discouragement from an apathetic culture; many of you may not expect to face this. This thirty-day guide through Scripture will remind you that you are not alone and that God is more concerned with your obedience than with others' reactions.

There are many books that are designed to be read in one

sitting or at your own pace. Even though you could sit and read this book from cover to cover and be benefited, I believe you would not receive the full benefit of what is being offered if you do that. Part One is designed to be read as you would read any book. These ten chapters can be read at your own pace and at any point before your mission trip begins. It would be most beneficial if you read all the chapters prior to your trip before you begin the thirty-day devotional.

Part Two is a thirty-day devotional that you need to begin reading thirty days before your trip so that you will finish the last devotion the day before you leave. Part Three is a thirty-day devotional that you need to begin reading on the last day of your mission trip as you are getting ready to travel home.

At the top of each devotional there is a title and suggested reading, followed by a Bible passage. In order to receive the full benefit of each devotional, I encourage you to have your Bible with you so you can read all of the suggested verses before you begin reading that day's devotional.

Only one devotional should be read each day to allow the reader to meditate, pray, and listen as the Holy Spirit reveals His truth. While it is possible to read multiple devotionals in one day, I believe that many truths might be overlooked and this book will not have the impact it was intended to have if you do that.

No matter how you choose to read this book though, I pray that it will deepen your walk with the Lord and will encourage and prepare you for your upcoming mission trip.

Part One

Lessons Learned

Chapter 1

Answered Prayer – Twenty-Three Years in the Making

You are a walking, breathing answered prayer. Someone somewhere has a need and has cried out to God. In His sovereignty, God has created and equipped you with the gifts and resources to help them. The reality is that you may not realize that your obedience will lead to a divine appointment between you, God, and a stranger. We can look to the Bible to see that God consistently answers prayers. Abraham waited twenty-five years for his promised son. The Israelites waited four hundred years to be delivered from their bondage. Hannah waited year after year for God to answer her prayer.

While there are times when it seems as if God is simply going to remain silent, other times His response is immediate. Isaiah's prayer for cleansing, a leper's prayer for healing, Peter's prayer to be saved from drowning, and Elijah's prayer for fire to come down from heaven received immediate responses. Those who repent and place their trust in Christ also receive an immediate response from God. It is not for us to know how or when things will happen in our lives, but it is our responsibility to trust that God is in control. Isaiah 60:22 says, *I, the LORD, will hasten it in its time.*

I was halfway through my eleven-day mission trip to Thailand when I discovered that our presence was an answer to a twenty-three-year-old prayer. The missionary, Cheri, grew up in a Baptist church in western Kentucky as a preacher's kid. She had spent the last twenty-three years on the mission field. Much of that time had been in northern Thailand. I will never forget the day she shared with our team that she had been praying for the last twenty-three years that God would send a mission team from her local Baptist association in western Kentucky. We were not only the first mission team to come from her hometown in the United States, but we were also able to continue to minister to the Hmong people of Thailand even after her family was led back to the States. God heard her voice and her heart's cry, and He orchestrated our arrival with her family's departure to create a flawless transition. We were the answer to a twenty-three-year-old prayer.

God is sovereign, and we will never fully know why He does what He does when He does it. One possible reason why God made Abraham wait twenty-five years for the son He promised him was because Abraham may not have been ready to be the father of the nation of Israel. God used those two and a half decades to teach Abraham patience and faithfulness and to help him develop the qualities necessary to effectively father the nation of Israel.

You may not recognize what God is doing right now, but there is no question He is molding you for His good purpose. Let this truth sink in: *You* are the answer to someone's prayer. It could be a family in a village located in the remotest part of the earth, or your neighbor across the street. God may use you in ways you never imagined, and you may never even know it. There are people all over the world who are lost and are praying for answers, as well as missionaries who are exhausted and are praying for help. God has the answer, and the answer might just be you.

Chapter 2

Planes, Trains, and Automobiles – Enjoy the Journey

One of the surprisingly difficult things that people are unaware of when they sign up for a mission trip is the amount of travel that is involved. Obviously, it will depend on your mission team's destination; nevertheless, the travel time and experience will be more than most people expect. My first mission trip included a three-hour flight to Newark, a nine-hour flight to Rio de Janeiro, a two-hour taxi ride, and a four-hour bus ride into the mountains. On one of my last trips to Thailand, I was on four different planes and spent more than twenty-four hours in the air. Every day consisted of about two hours in a van traveling to different villages, and two hours back to our hotel room each night. It has been my experience that when you are looking for people who have very limited access to the gospel, it will take longer to reach them.

In 2014, I traveled to the Philippines to work with a missionary named Michael. We spent a week in Manila and traveled to several villages on the mainland, but first we flew down to one of the many islands to disciple a small group of new believers in Busuanga and Coron. I had to take three planes and travel more than thirty hours to reach Manila, where I met Michael.

We got up early to catch another small plane that was heading down to Coron. As we approached the airport, I noticed twenty or thirty cows encompassing the runway. It wasn't your typical runway, but looked as if concrete had been poured in sections – something someone might do for a driveway. We had to circle the airport a couple of times until the cattle moved off the runway. Once we landed, it seemed as if we had entered a different world. The air was humid, and it smelled like chicken farms back in Kentucky. The airport was an oversized pavilion like you would see at your city park. One side was for arrivals and the other side was for departures. Good luck if you were traveling without a translator because there were no signs or announcements in English that would normally be at larger airports. We were greeted by a gentleman who hosted us for the next few days. We hopped into the back of his jeep and spent at least four hours bouncing along some of the roughest terrain I have ever been on – which is saying quite a lot for a rural Kentucky boy. Even though we had left Michael's house first thing in the morning, we did not arrive at our destination/home/hut/church plant until ten o'clock at night.

My body physically ached and my mind was almost numb from the experience. To be honest, I was looking forward to rolling out my sleeping bag and getting some much-needed rest, but as we hopped off the jeep, I soon realized that the villagers there were ready for us to start teaching. It was ten o'clock at night! There was no electricity. The only light was one lantern and the millions of stars that lit up the sky. I taught through the translator for two hours. However, as I was teaching, more people simply appeared out of the darkness. First there was a mother and her child. Then an older man with a cane arrived. They were so hungry to hear the Word of God that it made every bump, every security check, every cramped airplane seat, and the endless hours of stiffness and restlessness fully worth it.

What I have learned from this aspect of short-term mission service is that you must enjoy the journey. You will face challenges along the way. There will be layovers, delays, crowded bus rides that prevent sleep, jet lag that will make you feel as if you have been hit by a ton of bricks, and you may feel exhausted before you even start.

However, I promise that once you get to where God is sending you, you will be given renewed strength. You will see God do amazing and unexplainable things that you will never forget. You will begin to understand just how much God blesses those who are obedient. Breathe. Sit back. Relax. Try to rest. Most importantly, take in the scenery, marvel at God's majestic creation, and be confident in knowing that God is preparing the hearts of every person you will encounter on your trip.

In addition to embracing the physical and mental challenges of your journey, there are some vital truths to keep in mind. Your mission trip started when you accepted Christ as your Lord and Savior. Every day you are encountering people who are lost and are in need of someone to share the good news of Jesus Christ with them. The person sitting next to you on the plane for nine hours may be lost. The family in the airport has been placed in your terminal at your gate for a specific reason. The driver of your bus or taxi has been divinely placed in your path for a reason. Do not wait until you arrive at your destination to "transform" into a missionary. If you are a follower of Jesus, then you have been called to fish for men.

In 2011, I was on a mission trip to Puerto Rico, and we had a fifteen-year-old boy named Keneth as our translator. He rode with us everywhere we went and served as our navigator and voice to the local villagers. The interesting thing about Keneth was that unlike many translators I have worked with in the past, Keneth was not a believer. Day after day he would translate the story of the death, burial, and resurrection of Jesus Christ. He saw many people trust Christ as their Lord and Savior, but he was still lost and confused.

All week long as we drove from one location to the next, I would talk with Keneth. I used our three-hour round trip to explain the Bible and answer questions. When the week ended, I did not want to leave. There was work waiting to be done, but it was time to go. Only a week or two later, I got a message on Facebook from Keneth telling me that he had given his life to the Lord. I was so excited to hear the news! What a beautiful reminder that every small gospel conversation we have on the journey to and from our destinations could bear eternal fruit! I look forward to seeing my brother in Christ again one day.

Another important lesson to remember is that jet lag is real. Jet lag is when your body's internal clock does not match up with the time zone you are in. There are several symptoms that you may experience, including fatigue, headaches, lack of concentration, being sleepy during the day, and having insomnia at night. These symptoms may only last a day, or they may last the entire week. As such, we need to try our best to acclimate to our new time zone the best we can.

I am going to share with you some of the things that have helped me battle jet lag. The day we start traveling, I check the time of my final destination and start operating on their schedule. If it is daytime at my destination, then I will force myself to stay awake on my flight. I walk around the cabin, and if I get really sleepy, I take short fifteen-minute naps. However, if it is nighttime at my destination, then I will try my best to sleep on the flight over – even if it is in the middle of the day where I am. Melatonin is a supplement that people use as a sleep aid, but its main purpose is to regulate your internal clock. Remember to always consult your doctor before using any supplement. I typically take some melatonin the first few nights I am overseas to help my body adjust to the new time zone. Also, your body is trying to figure out when it needs to eat, so it is beneficial to eat several small meals and snacks throughout the day. None of these are a guaranteed cure for jet lag, but all of these suggestions may help you feel better as you seek to serve God wherever He has called you.

Remember that the journey is part of the mission, and you should try to physically prepare your body. Never forget that God has wonderful blessings in store for those who are obedient. In short, do not disregard the joy of the journey – even if you face extreme challenges.

Chapter 3

Tylenol – Knowing When You Need Help

I love movies, and one of the most common storylines in many movies is the reluctant spy. Somehow an ordinary person or average family is caught in the middle of a potential rogue CIA agent and a shadow syndicate. Writers and movie producers take an everyday citizen who has no business being involved, and they send him into the lion's den with nothing but an audio wire and a safe word. Thank God for the safe word. This is a word you can utter that will alert those listening that you are in over your head. You are in trouble; the enemy has discovered your secret, and it is time to send in the calvary. *Tylenol*, as strange as it may sound, is my ministry safe word.

It is important for everyone on your team to know their physical and emotional limitations. I know that admitting a weakness goes against every fiber of our being. We are not wired to show vulnerability – especially if we are in positions of leadership, but there is no biblical evidence to support such behavior. There are several examples in the Bible when leaders struggle, and the support of those around them allows them to be successful. Moses became physically weak during the battle against the Amalekites, but Aaron and Hur stood beside him and held up his arms until the enemy was defeated (Exodus 17:12).

A chapter later we find Moses trying to judge the disputes of the entire nation of Israel. Jethro said to him:

> The thing that you are doing is not good. You will surely wear out, both yourself and these people who are with you, for the task is too heavy for you; you cannot do it alone. Now listen to me, I will give you counsel, and God be with you. You be the people's representative before God, and you bring the disputes to God, then teach them the statues and the laws, and make known to them the way in which they are to walk and the work they are to do. Furthermore, you shall select out of all the people able men who fear God, men of truth, those who hate dishonest gain; and you shall place these over them as leaders of thousands, of hundreds, of fifties and of tens. (Exodus 18:17-21)

The truth does not only apply to leaders, but also to every believer. Galatians 6:2 says, *Bear one another's burdens, and thereby fulfill the law of Christ.* It does not matter if you are a team member or a team leader. None of us are all-powerful or all-knowing. We have our limitations, and it is okay to acknowledge them by asking for help. God created us to be rational creatures both toward Him and His church. We are not meant to serve Him in isolation. Do not be so arrogant as to think that you are the exception. Peter was confident that he had enough faith to walk out onto the water, but it was not long before he began to sink because he took his eyes off Jesus. His legs and waist started to melt into the waves; he was in trouble. The only thing left to do was to cry out his safe words, *Lord, save me!* (Matthew 14:30).

In 2011, I went as a team member to Villalba and Ponce in Puerto Rico as part of an initiative with the Kentucky Baptist Convention. The next year I led my first overseas mission trip back to Puerto Rico in hopes of forming a partnership. There were many things that went right and even more that went wrong, but what I remember the most was that I had to cry out, "Tylenol."

We had been there for two days and were staying in Mayaguez on the west coast when I felt as if my head was going to explode. I worked all day cleaning up the property of the local church, and by that evening I knew I had a full-blown sinus infection. I had to rely on my team to proceed without me as I lay in the hotel room praying that the antibiotic would kick in and that the Lord would provide me with a quick recovery. The next day I was healthy enough to get back in the field. If I had pretended that everything was okay, I would have hindered the ministry. It would not have been brave or courageous to refuse medicine, treatment, or rest. The team's success did not depend on me, but on God.

It is okay to admit that Father Time has caught up with you and not make the journey up the mountain with the rest of the team. It will be okay if you hear devastating news from home and need an afternoon alone in God's Word. There is nothing to be embarrassed about when your stomach is having a hard time handling the local cuisine. When you go on a mission trip, your body is in a constant state of adapting. You are tired from the time change, dehydrated from the heat, cold from the altitude, queasy from the food, and mentally drained from being bombarded with so many new things.

Responding to these pressures is normal. You are not a failure, and there is no shame in crying out your safe word when you have reached your limit. You are not God, and the sooner you realize this truth, the better off you will be.

Chapter 4

Apes Together Strong –
The Importance of Team Unity

A new *Planet of the Apes* adaptation hit the theaters in 2011. One phrase that is used throughout every movie by Caesar, the leader and first elder of the apes, is "Apes together strong." In each storyline we find the humans and the apes living in relative peace until one or two individuals are determined to sow dissension. At the height of the conflict, Caesar raised his two fists in the air and brought everyone together. He shouted the famous line, "Apes together strong." It was a reminder to everyone who could hear him that alone they were weak, vulnerable, easy to control, and unable to defeat the enemy, but together they would be unstoppable.

I remember a scene from the third installment when the apes had been captured and were living in a prison encampment. Caesar had run off earlier in the movie to avenge his family, but he had found himself in the same situation as everyone else. He lay in the mud beaten and defeated, separated from the rest of his tribe, when a little human girl whom he had rescued approached him and showed him kindness. She did the same for the other prisoners, and as Caesar looked up he saw the symbol of unity begin to form above the head of every ape. The unity of his people had been destroyed, and it seemed as though the enemy had won. Even so, there was still hope, but it required them to work together.

I am here to tell you that you will face adversity on your mission trip because anytime you are striving to be obedient to what God has called you to do, there will be opposition. You will be with your team twenty-four hours a day for one to two weeks, and it is inevitable that you will encounter drama. The cramped bus rides and the snoring roommate will no longer be fun stories, but an irritation. The jokes your team members make that were once funny have lost their flavor. People begin to complain and grumble under their breath. Feelings get hurt and, like an infection, division begins to spread. It only takes one or two individuals to destroy a team's unity, and many times it occurs by accident without any evil intent. Nevertheless, the damage has been done, and the team struggles to be joyful and effective.

One trip I was leading was made up of so many strong and unique personalities that I was not sure how cohesive the team was going to be. A couple of days into the week, the tension between the members was undeniable. One person would complain about every decision that was made. Another would run off and hide when any work needed to be done. It was starting to affect the group. Every night I would leave the rest of the team to travel an hour and half away to teach at a pastor's conference, and on the third night, after we had returned from the conference, I was summoned over to the rest of the team. One of our ladies had recognized the rising tension and decided to teach a couple of nightly devotions. She opened the Word of God, prayed over the team, and began the process of restoring unity. She helped them to see that they were divided, but that together they could be strong. It did not take much to restore unity, and while it was not a permanent fix, it allowed God to work freely through our team, and we had a successful trip.

God loves unity, and He tells us this when He says, *Behold how good and how pleasant it is for brothers to dwell together in unity! It is like the precious oil upon the head, coming down upon the beard, even Aaron's beard, coming down upon the edge of his robes. It is like the dew of Hermon coming down upon the mountains of Zion; for there the* LORD *commanded the blessing – life forever* (Psalm 133:1-3). Unity is both good and pleasant, and just as anointing oil poured upon the head creates a pleasant atmosphere and gives refreshment, unity renews the spirit of God's people. Oil running down into the beard and eventually falling upon the robe paints the picture of the rich and abundant blessing that accompanies spiritual unity of fellow believers. It is a wonderful thing when God's children come together for God's purpose, but wherever God is at work, you can guarantee that Satan will be there to try to destroy what God has created.

We see an example of this opposition when Nehemiah unified the nation of Israel in an effort to rebuild the wall and gates of Jerusalem. It was not long after construction began that Sanballat and his friends began to threaten the people of Israel, trying to deter them from their task. Another example is when Moses attempted to maintain unity among the two million Israelites traveling to the promised land, but at every turn it seemed that there was someone who tried to create divisions among the people. At one point they turned to Aaron and built a golden calf. Later they attempted to appoint a leader and return to Egypt (Numbers 14:1-4). Even in a small group of twelve disciples chosen by Jesus, we find Judas questioning the things that Jesus was doing, and he eventually betrayed Him.

So what is the lesson? We are to strive for unity that will allow us to work in cooperation with one another for the glory of God. We are to be mindful that there will be opposition and obstacles that will try to disrupt the team harmony. We do not need to be afraid to confront difficult issues or confess sinful attitudes, because unresolved team drama leads to an unsuccessful trip. Do not allow the "Sanballats" and "Judases" of the world to frustrate what God is doing within you and your team. God created us to be relational creatures – both in relation to Him and each other. So remember that we are better together: Christians together strong!

Chapter 5

Of Course You Did – Finding an Open Door

I f you could be anyone, be yourself – unless, of course, you could be Kevin. That name might not mean anything to you, but to me it is the name of a fellow pastor and good friend whom I had the privilege of serving alongside in Thailand. This was our team's first trip to Thailand in search of an unreached people group that we could begin to pray for and minister to. There were six of us on the trip, and by the end of our week and a half together, we all laughed when we heard the phrase, "Of course you did, Kevin."

Kevin is a man of many talents, and he was not afraid to use every previous life experience to make connections with everyone we interacted with while we were in Thailand. He always tried to find an open door, make a connection, and share the good news of Jesus Christ. He truly encompassed 1 Corinthians 9:19-23:

> Though I am free from all men, I have made myself a slave to all, so that I may win more. To the Jews I became as a Jew, so that I might win Jews; to those who are under the Law, as under the Law though

not being myself under the Law, so that I might
win those who are under the Law; to those who
are without law, as without law, though not being
without the law of God but under the law of Christ,
so that I might win those who are without law.
To the weak I became weak, that I might win the
weak; I have become all things to all men, so that I
may by all means save some. I do all things for the
sake of the gospel, so that I may become a fellow
partaker of it.

We had just arrived in Bangkok, and one of the missionaries
was there waiting to take us to our hotel. His name was David,
and on the drive from the airport to the hotel Kevin had already
established that they had grown up in the same town and both
had experience hog farming. While you are unable to see my
face as I write this, I could not stop my eyes from rolling as I
typed that last sentence. I did not think anything of it at the
time, but I learned that Kevin just had a special way of con-
necting with people.

Another time we were sitting in a classroom full of Hmong
seminary students in Udon, Thailand. I picked up a guitar, while
Jody, another team member, sat behind the drums – and here
comes Dr. Kevin walking up behind the keyboard. I had used
my guitar talents on many occasions in our local association
of churches, but I was surprised to learn that, of course, Kevin
could play the guitar *and* the piano.

We were on a bus in Laos heading back into Thailand, and
Kevin happened to be standing next to the only English-speaking
person on the bus. This young woman was from Wells, England,
which just happened to be where Kevin finished his doctorate
degree. He was able to use that connection to talk to her about

her spiritual beliefs and to share the gospel. As I heard this, I thought, *Kevin spent time in England? Of course you did, Kevin.*

Later, one of the leaders of the seminary was talking about the need for some type of computer program that could help the Hmong-speaking students understand difficult terms – something like a digital thesaurus. Of course, Kevin had already written a program that he believed would do the job.

Another time we were sitting in the home of a local Hmong family, and the head of the household was sharing the story of spiritual warfare and how his father did not get past a certain grade level due to circumstances in his life. As we listened to his story, Kevin responded by saying, "My dad also had to quit school at that same age." The group almost said the words in unison: "Of course you did, Kevin." We laughed and had a fun time, and Kevin was a great sport, but the reality was that he was embodying the lesson of becoming all things to all people. He listened to people and found shared experiences, gifts, resources, and talents that he could use to make connections and glorify God.

Accept Paul's challenge in 1 Corinthians 9 and be like Kevin. You may think that you do not have enough talent or experiences to connect with complete strangers, but God did not make a mistake when He called you to the mission field. He chose you. He designed you. He knows your past experiences and your current circumstances. He has orchestrated every encounter you will have and has opened doors of opportunity for you to proclaim the good news of Jesus Christ. Look for the open door, make a connection, and share the gospel.

Kevin would not want me to tell you to imitate him, but instead to be a reflection of Christ. Paul tells us in 1 Corinthians 11:1, *Be imitators of me, just as I also am of Christ.* It is okay to look at the examples of others when that person is living in such a way that helps us become more like Christ. I gave Kevin a hard time about all the connections that he made while we were in Thailand, but he reminded me that there is always an open door for ministry if we are willing to look for it. Do not get so caught up in the itinerary or the big speaking engagements that you forget to make those interpersonal connections that open doors to gospel conversation. Be the team member who turns every encounter into a Jesus encounter.

Chapter 6

Puzzle Pieces – God Is in Control

You have decided to go on a mission trip and share the good news of Jesus Christ with the world. It does not matter if you are going to a neighboring state or the other side of the world; you need to understand that you are simply one piece to an extremely large and complex puzzle. You may have assembled the edge pieces and have an idea of what is going on and what is expected of you. However, it is more likely that you are completely clueless and are just following the directions of your team leader.

Let me guess. You were at church one Sunday when a team that just returned from their foreign mission trip walked up on stage to give their report. It was filled with wonderful stories and heart-melting pictures of children showing love to the team members. The team was very excited, and they laughed as they spoke about how they grew closer to God and to one another. At the end of the presentation, they encouraged the congregation to join the next team, and they placed a sheet of paper at the front of the sanctuary. Before you realized it, your name was on the list and you were sitting on a plane ready for takeoff.

I am sure your story has its variations, but the results are the same – you are off to take the gospel to the nations. You are not joining this mission trip by accident. God is all knowing, and no decision you make is a surprise to Him. He has a plan and purpose for you on this trip that fits into His perfectly designed strategy. It is unfortunate that we do not get to witness God putting all the pieces together, but on the rare occasion that He allows us to see what He is doing, it is beautiful.

Our local association of churches had a vision to take the gospel to an unreached people group and disciple their pastors and church leaders for effective ministry. The goal was to find a people group that had limited-to-no access to the gospel or Scripture in their language and to develop a discipleship program that would train pastors. We prayed for God to send us to the right country and the right people, but it seemed that God closed every door we tried to open.

There was a missionary in Thailand who was connected to one of our local churches. It just so happened that Jody, a local pastor, who first brought the vision to the leadership of our association, was serving at the church the missionary Cheri's father once pastored. Later that year we flew over to Thailand, and with Cheri as our guide, we fell in love with the Hmong people. I was asked to lead a team in 2020. Our main objective was to find a local believer whom we could support and develop to be our hands and feet in Thailand year-round. To find a Hmong, Thai, and English-speaking believer in an unfamiliar country filled with seventy-one million people, only 150,000 of whom are Hmong, seemed like an impossible task. So I made the only possible choice I could make: I prayed.

Only a week or so later I was standing in the local middle school talking to one of the teachers after leading the morning Bible study for the students when God connected a puzzle piece. I was sharing with her the challenge that was placed before me when she interrupted and said that she might be able to help.

A missionary whom her church supported in Thailand had just given a presentation, and she remembered hearing the word "Hmong." A quick email to southeast Thailand led me to Minnesota, then to Chiang Mai, and eventually to a man in northern Thailand named Gideon. The trip was a success, and Gideon was the perfect fit – but God was not done yet.

One of the team members from our first trip was a man named Kevin. You may remember him from the previous chapter, "Of Course You Did." Kevin knows a lot of people in many different areas of ministry with many different resources. He was able to find pastoral training material and the funding to get it translated. The only thing that we still needed that he could not supply was time.

Fast forward to March 2020, just a few weeks after my trip to Thailand. The COVID pandemic began to wreak havoc on the world. We were unable to travel to Thailand for almost two years, but God had given us the one thing we needed: time to translate the training material into Hmong. At the time of this publication, we are getting ready to do our first pastoral training conference teaching through the first book. The way in which this training came together could only have been done by the sovereign hand of God.

We never know what God is doing or how He is working behind the scenes. He already has everything planned out, and all He needs from us is obedience. Paul tells us in Ephesians 1:11 that in Jesus *we have obtained an inheritance, having been predestined according to His purpose who works all things after the counsel of His will.* God has a plan, and everything will play out exactly as He has foreseen. We do not need to worry if we do not know every detail about where we are going or what we are doing. We do not need to be arrogant and think that we have all the answers and that there will be no surprises. We simply need to be obedient and trust that God is in control.

In 2014, I had a wonderful plan to start a partnership with a missionary in a foreign country. I did not know where to begin, so I started asking everyone I knew who had connections to overseas missions. My Aunt Teresa called me and told me about a couple who were members of her church who had been missionaries in the Philippines for the past ten years. It was not long after that conversation that I was on a plane to meet Michael and his family. I will spare you the details, but it was an amazing trip. The search was over. I was going back to my church to tell them that we needed to partner with Michael in the Philippines.

Providentially, God had different plans. The lead pastor was not on board. Then Michael and his family had to move back to the States. I was confused. God was definitely doing something. How did I get it so wrong? Five years later, after having accepted a senior pastor position at another church, I was looking for an overseas missions' partner. My friend Michael was now in Honduras serving alongside Sam, and let me say that this connection was ordained. We have been in partnership with Sam for more than five years now.

I thought I had it figured out. The answer seemed obvious to me, but I could not see what God was doing. I only had a few pieces of the puzzle and was trying to make them fit together. As I look back over the last few years, there is no denying that I was supposed to meet Michael. It just was not the right time, the right church, the right country, or the right ministry at first. God was moving all the pieces into place, and after He snapped them together, it was so satisfying to step back and look at what He had been doing the entire time.

God has you where you are for a reason. You might be a Jody who has a vision, a Kevin who has the connections, or a school teacher at a middle school who can connect a puzzle piece, but no matter who you are, God has a plan and purpose for your obedience. He is moving pieces into place so that you and your team can be effective on the mission field. Trust what God is doing and listen to the guidance of the Holy Spirit. If God closes a door, do not try to force it open.

There is a reason for everything that God chooses to do or not do. Our job is simply to be obedient. We try to make everything complicated, but the truth is that trusting God is simple. The world may seem big, but compared to God it is microscopic. God can find the one perfectly gifted individual from a group of seventy-one million. He can move a missionary 9,800 miles across the globe from Manila to Tegucigalpa. He can and has chosen you and has a purpose for you that you have yet to discover. Remember, *God causes all things to work together for good to those who love God, to those who are called according to His purpose* (Romans 8:28). If you are following God's call and serving Him in love, then rest assured that everything will work out exactly as God planned.

Chapter 7

Walking Among Giants –
Gaining Spiritual Perspective

It would be a mistake to think that just because you are the one going on a mission trip that you are the teacher and not the student. I feel as if I have learned more about who God is and what He is doing from the spiritual giants whom I have encountered over the years than I have ever taught anyone else.

For example, it was on an island between the South China and Sulu Seas when I experienced what true hunger for God's Word looked like. God used a little girl named Seven in Ontario, Canada, to teach me gratitude as she wept when I gave her my Bible. I felt true generosity in the mountains of Thailand as a man brought out every blanket he owned so we would stay warm during the night, while keeping very little for himself or his wife. I and two others were staying in an orphanage that was in the process of being built in Russia. Our host told us the story about the lady who saw a great need and poured everything she had into constructing the orphanage that would one day not only rescue children who had been abandoned but would also be a center for the gospel of Jesus Christ. The government did not like the idea of a Christian orphanage being built and so snuck into her home one night and beat her within an inch of her life. She moved away but continued her work at the orphanage from a secret location. This was true persistence and sacrifice.

You have a great opportunity to proclaim the good news of Jesus Christ to people all over the world who will come just to hear what the Americans have to say, but what you will find is that your faith will grow as you walk alongside these battle-tested missionaries and believers.

It was 2007. Communism had officially been removed from Russia since 1992, but unofficially the ideas and attitudes still lived in the hearts of many of the people and leaders. The relationship toward Americans and Christianity has been a roller-coaster relationship for decades. We were in Klintsy, Russia, meeting with believers and proclaiming salvation through Jesus to as many people as we could, but we found that because of the lingering hostility toward Christians, our options were limited. We were not allowed to gather in public places to preach the gospel or travel door-to-door in hopes of having gospel conversations. Therefore, the plan was for the local believers to go into their neighborhoods and invite everyone to come to their homes or local church building to hear from the American believers. On most occasions we were able to meet with two or three people and share our testimony and the plan of salvation. However, it was not the encounters with the unbelieving that stood out in my mind, but the conversations with the faithful Christians who were living in daily obedience.

One evening we arrived at the home of a local Christian couple who were probably in their eighties. We waited for their friends and neighbors to arrive, but no one showed up. It was a God-ordained moment because we were able to sit down with them for the next hour and hear about their spiritual journey. They lived during the height of oppression from a Communist government that would destroy people's livelihood or even take their lives because of their faith.

They recalled stories of sneaking through town at night to meet in secret with other believers. They remembered how uplifting those meetings were, how they fervently prayed over one another, and how they made sure that everyone was being cared for. It reminded me of the Christians in the book of Acts during the first century. Yes, it was difficult and dangerous to live in obedience, but it was a life filled with joy, blessings, and fulfillment.

They talked about the fall of Communism and the freedom they gained to worship on Sunday mornings in public church buildings. At first it was wonderful, but I soon realized that it was one of the worst things that happened to the Christian faith in Russia. During the time when Christians were facing religious persecution in Russia, one knew the genuineness of a person's faith by the simple fact that they showed up to a Bible study. They were taking a huge risk, and if they were caught, they could lose their jobs and their ability to provide for their families. They could be imprisoned or even killed because of their faith. It created a bond among the believers as they relied fully on Christ and each other. It was a modern-day picture of Acts 2:44: *And all those who had believed were together and had all things in common.*

Once Communism fell in 1992, everyone was allowed to gather at the church on Sunday and they had to risk nothing. The authenticity of their faith began to falter, and their relationships with other believers became superficial. They did not know who the true followers of Christ were and who were using the worship time as a social gathering. It was discouraging to many of the believers to watch their once strong and vibrant church become corrupted by a complacent and convenient faith. These spiritual giants who knew more about risk, sacrifice, perseverance, prayer, and genuine fellowship than I will ever know taught me a lesson in true faithfulness that I have never forgotten.

I do not want to discredit the sacrifice you are making to serve God wherever He may be calling you, but in many ways, it pales in comparison to what other believers suffer because of their faith each day. Watch as the local believers teach you about being content or joyful in the face of insurmountable odds. Learn the definition of dedication as these villagers walk for miles after working in the fields all week just to attend church or a Bible study. Ask yourself if you would be as joyful as the single mom with two kids living in a one-room shed whose only treasure is her relationship with God. Yes, you *have been approved by God to be entrusted with the gospel* (1 Thessalonians 2:4) and appointed to proclaim, *Repent and believe* (Mark 1:15) wherever you may go. As you do, be sure to keep your eyes, ears, and heart open to receive the lessons from the many spiritual giants of the faith you will encounter along the way.

Chapter 8

The Danger Is Real –
The Reality of Spiritual Warfare

Spiritual warfare will present itself in many different forms and attack on several different fronts. It will become more evident the moment you recognize the voice of God calling you to go on a mission trip. There may be a financial crisis that will cause you to question your ability to afford the trip. You may receive some difficult news about your health that makes you nervous about how safe it is for you to travel. Your coworkers, boss, and family may cause you to feel guilty for taking a week to follow God's call on your life. All of these situations and many others challenge our resolve and test our faith.

We need to remember what God's Word says: *All who desire to live godly in Christ Jesus will be persecuted* (2 Timothy 3:12). Peter reminds us of this again, telling us, *Do not be surprised at the fiery ordeal among you, which comes upon you for your testing, as though some strange thing were happening to you; but to the degree that you share the sufferings of Christ, keep on rejoicing* (1 Peter 4:12-13).

When you decide to take a leap of faith and sign up for that overseas mission trip, then do not think for one second that

Satan will sit back and do nothing. He will do whatever he can to disrupt your life and lead you into disobedience. These attacks may be physical, emotional, or spiritual. They may come from people we trust and care about, or they may be internal struggles of fear, guilt, or anxiety. Even though spiritual warfare may intensify when you are contemplating going on a mission trip, Satan is always creating obstacles that faithful followers of Christ will have to overcome. It is my experience that the more challenges, detours, and complications I had to face leading up to my trip, the greater the work that God was getting ready to do through and in me.

You must also be aware that spiritual warfare is not just a deterrent to the preparation of what God is about to do, but it is rather a continuous effort to frustrate God's plan. However, God's Word tells us, *The LORD of hosts has planned, and who can frustrate it? And as for His stretched-out hand, who can turn it back?* (Isaiah 14:27). God's purpose is set and His will is predetermined, and there is no one who is able to disrupt what God is going to do. Because Satan is always at work against us, we must expect that the spiritual warfare we have encountered will not cease once we get on the plane to our destination, but will persist and may even intensify.

Many of the things you may face have already been mentioned in earlier chapters. There is the constant struggle to maintain strong team dynamics and unity. You may face fatigue, dehydration, jet lag, and digestive issues. You may encounter political tensions and hostility toward the Christian faith. I have seen team members serve with great excitement during the first half of the week, but one phone call from home caused them to revert into their comfort zone. Sometimes the attacks seem like everyday occurrences that no one would consider spiritual warfare, and other times they are very direct and obvious.

We were on our way to a small village in Russia that was

located on the border of Ukraine and Belarus. Because we were foreigners, the Russian government would not allow us to visit any town on the border unless we had prior approval two weeks in advance. This was a fact that we did not learn until we arrived at the police station to place our request. Since the entirety of the trip was two weeks, there was not enough time to get approval before it would be time to leave. We were respectful of the rules and regulations and made plans to have everyone in the village meet us at a local church in a neighboring town that we were allowed to visit. The local authorities did not think that we would adhere to their laws and sent police officers to arrest us if we attempted to enter the border village.

Satan was working as hard as he could to disrupt what God had planned. The previous day, our team leader got mysteriously sick and spent the whole day at the hospital. He was with us while we were adapting and relocating, but he was very weak. We were under attack by local police, physical sickness, and challenges to find a place to freely share the gospel. I am happy to report that it ended up being the best night of the trip. People from the street slowly and continuously filled the small church building. Our team leader preached with such a strong conviction and boldness that several people trusted Christ as their Lord and Savior. I remember how weak our team leader had been just moments before he started preaching and how healthy and vibrant he looked as he explained the gospel. Then I saw him almost collapse in exhaustion after he finished, as if God alone had empowered him to accomplish His good purpose through preaching.

It is an undeniable fact that all who choose to live a godly life will face persecution and will need to be ready to stand against the spiritual forces of darkness and wickedness. It is also true that God has clothed us in godly armor and goes with us through the fire (Isaiah 43:2). He promises that He will be with us and that He will never leave us nor forsake us (Hebrews 13:5). God is sovereign, omnipotent, omniscient, and always present. His will is absolute and cannot be influenced or frustrated. We fight a defeated enemy. Revelation 20:10 says, *And the devil who deceived them was thrown into the lake of fire and brimstone, where the beast and the false prophet are also; and they will be tormented day and night forever and ever.*

Do not get discouraged if money gets tight; God will provide. Do not walk away if you feel as if you are not physically able to go; God will strengthen and heal. Do not let your fear, anxiety, and guilt keep you from serving; God will sustain you. Do not worry about the possible obstacles you may face; God will protect you. Spiritual warfare is a reality, but God is victorious.

Chapter 9

Active Listening –
Always Listen to the Missionary

What is safe to eat? Where is it safe to go? What is safe to say? When do I need to rest? What type of clothes should I wear? These are just a few of the questions that need to be answered before and during your mission trip. Yes, you can do a Google search and learn general facts about your destination. You might even get a few tips on the local cuisine or popular sites to visit. The problem is that when you are on a mission trip and are traveling into locations away from the tourist scene, things become a lot more dangerous. You are entering into a culture and a world that does not cater to travelers and their wallets. You are encountering everyday people living their everyday lives, and no matter how much research you do before you go, you will need a guide. The missionaries you are working with, who live, speak, eat, and know the culture, will be your most valuable resource. They will help you react to the things you encounter. They will be your voice when there is a language barrier. They may very well be the reason you are allowed to get on or off the plane. You should always listen to your missionaries.

My first foreign mission trip was to Brazil when I was seventeen years old. I traveled with thirty other people, and I was the only one under the age of thirty on the trip. They paired me with a young pastor and youth pastor and sent us up to the mountains. We were supposed to work in the mountains for a week and then head back down to Rio de Janeiro for a couple days of sightseeing.

The local pastor and missionary with whom we were working wanted us to do some discipleship in one of his churches in Rio, so while everyone else was enjoying the first day of sightseeing, we headed off with our missionary into the inner city. As we approached the church, a man with a sawed-off shotgun stepped in front of the car and pointed his gun right at the windshield. I remember our missionary reaching up and turning on the interior light of the car and telling us to show them our hands. He reached out of the car window and pointed to the church down the road. The man looked inside the car, lowered his gun, and smiled really big. He began talking with the missionary as if they were best friends. We were never in any real danger because of the relationships and the respect that had been established by our missionary. He knew where it was safe to go, he knew how to respond when we entered gang territory, and he had built a reputation to navigate the culture.

It was at that moment that I understood how important it was to trust my host missionary, the person whom God had called and assigned to a particular culture and people group. My effectiveness and my safety were intimately connected to the missionary I was serving alongside.

There are so many stories that I could share that would emphasize this important lesson. There was the time I went to Russia and learned that there were different levels of presenting the gospel that depended on a village's exposure to Christianity and the tolerance of the local authority to share publicly. It was in the Philippines that my missionary friend Michael taught me the importance of rest. It was so hot and humid in that secluded village on the long island that even with my diligence in staying hydrated, I found myself physically exhausted. Michael looked at me and simply told me to go drink an entire bottle of water and take a nap. He knew that I was not used to this type of heat and that I was losing more water even while I was sleeping than I was taking in during the day. He understood what was happening, and he took care of me.

My missionary friend Sam taught me to be vigilant when eating the local food, and our missionary in Russia constantly reminded me to never drink water that was not in a sealed bottle or any drink that had ice cubes in it because of bacteria in the local water. In the Philippines, there were certain types of shirts that pastors wore and that I was to wear so that when I was teaching, the locals would recognize my role and be respectful. Certain colors of clothing, such as red and blue, were prohibited in Memphis due to gang activity. There were a couple of Caribbean islands where it was dangerous to wear camouflage due to military tension. Also, some of our female team members learned that there were particular types of clothing that needed to be worn in order to be culturally appropriate and allow our team access to particular people groups that we might come in contact with on our trip.

I am very thankful for every missionary whom I have had the honor to serve alongside. They have given their entire lives to serve God in some of the most difficult places in the world. They have kept me safe, kept me healthy, helped me to understand the culture, showed me how to be respectful, and taught me how to proclaim the gospel with clarity to people I did not understand. If I was allowed to give only one piece of advice to people going on their first mission trip, it would be, "Always listen to your missionary."

Chapter 10

The Hardships of Coming Home

The decision to step out of your comfort zone and go on a mission trip is a challenging one. People question if they will be able to handle the airplane ride, the lack of comfortable accommodations, the different temperatures, and the language barrier. They worry if they will be able to handle the emotions that come with seeing children in an orphanage or the conditions that many people live in every day. It is difficult for them to leave a spouse at home to carry the weight of work and two kids with all of their school and sports activities.

These are all legitimate concerns, but what most people do not realize is that it is sometimes equally challenging to come home after you have been gone on a mission for a period of time. You have seen God do amazing things, and you are excited to share those stories with family and coworkers. You are motivated to proclaim the gospel to people in your church and community. You feel as if you are like Moses after he had experienced God at the burning bush, or like Paul, who after his encounter with Christ on the road to Damascus, truly had his eyes opened for the very first time.

As enthusiastic as you may be, there will be many people

who simply do not want to listen and do not care. There are many things that you will encounter that will discourage you and tempt you to return to life as normal instead of remaining joyful and obedient to the change that God has created in your heart.

There likely will be those people back home who lack hunger for the Word of God and are reluctant to obey its teaching – unlike my typical experiences with the believers overseas. There was a discipleship conference in the Philippines in which I taught for two hours (which would have been an hour too long at any church that I have served in the States), but they wanted me to continue teaching. They were so hungry for the Word of God that they would travel on foot for miles in the insufferable heat just so they could learn as much as they could about God's Word from complete strangers.

On another mission trip, a fellow pastor and friend were in Thailand teaching on church discipline in one of the villages. They began to ask very specific questions about how a church should go about approaching a brother in Christ who needed correction. As my friend was giving them guidance, they turned to one of the men in the room and began putting into action the truths of God's Word that they had just learned. They were eager to learn and be obedient.

When these experiences are so fresh and exciting to you, and then you return home and face an apathetic church, uninterested family members, and unreceptive coworkers, you realize that this reception coming home was a challenge you were not expecting to face.

I had just come back from a week of discipleship, vacation Bible school, and preaching in Puerto Rico when my pastor asked me to preach for our evening service. I arrived early to talk with the worship band and the audio-visual team about the Bible passages that they would be using so they could put them up on the screen. I did not know that the computer and PowerPoint were not working. The pastor, the worship leader, and the audio-visual team were all ready to cancel the service and send everyone home.

I was dumbfounded about the conversation they were having and began to think about my trip. I had just spent the last seven days in an open-air concrete building with no air conditioning and only one power outlet to run a small fan. The people sat in plastic chairs like those we would use in our backyards or on mats on the hard concrete floor. We did not have a computer with PowerPoint, or even hymnals. We had a guitar and the Bible, and only one of those was necessary. I walked up to the group at my church and simply said, "Turn it all off. We will be fine." These faithful church leaders were so used to (and took for granted) the conveniences of worship in a developed nation that they were distracted and failed to focus on what really mattered. You also may be tempted to rely on these conveniences and things that American Christianity says are necessary to be successful, but all we need is Jesus.

There will be constant temptation to leave your excitement, enthusiasm, and spiritual growth on the mission field. Your friends, coworkers, and maybe even other Christians will pressure you to fall in line and not disrupt the status quo. You will begin to think that they are right and that you can simply pick up on your next mission trip where you left off.

Do not listen to them! Stay strong! Paul tells us in Romans 12:1-2, *I urge you, brethren, by the mercies of God, to present your bodies a living and holy sacrifice, acceptable to God, which is your spiritual service of worship. And do not be conformed to this world, but be transformed by the renewing of your mind, so that you may prove what the will of God is, that which is good and acceptable and perfect.*

God will use you in some incredible ways on your trip, but

He does not want to stop there. His desire is for us to take up our cross daily and follow Him (Luke 9:23). He wants us to be *above reproach in the midst of a crooked and perverse generation, among whom you appear as lights in the world* (Philippians 2:15). God's Word tells us that we are called *out of darkness into His marvelous light* (1 Peter 2:9).

Please do not give up. Do not conform to the world. Remember who God is and that you belong to Him. Coming home may be more difficult than you realize, but you will not go through it alone.

Part Two

Thirty-Day Pre-Journey Devotional

Making the Ordinary Extraordinary

Acts 4:1-10

Now as they observed the confidence of Peter and
John and understood that they were uneducated
and untrained men, they were amazed, and began
to recognize them as having been with Jesus.
—Acts 4:13

The incredible factor in volunteerism is that God can take
ordinary people and help them overcome extraordinary
challenges. After Peter and John had turned the town upside
down with their preaching, they were rudely thrown in jail.
They rose to the occasion through the power of the Holy Spirit,
and they boldly preached the claims of Christ to the ones who
apprehended them.

When those who apprehended Peter and John saw their
courage and realized that they were unlearned and ignorant
men (some translations have *ordinary men*), they marveled and
took knowledge that they had been *with Jesus*. Regardless of your
background or training, God can and will use you. Spend time
with Jesus and develop a natural boldness to your witness. The
spiritual equation is this: one ordinary soul, plus God, equals
more than enough power to accomplish His purpose. Obey
with the courage that only Christ can provide!

Every day after our time in God's Word, we have a time of prayer. Each day we will be asked the same questions, and I pray that we will be honest with God as we respond. This devotional is your private time with God, and no one will read it unless you allow them to.

Day 2

Serve with a Team Spirit

Romans 12

Be devoted to one another in brotherly love; give preference to one another in honor.
—Romans 12:10

We go as volunteers ready to serve. We need committed servants rather than glory seekers, superstars, or prima donnas. We do not need "lone rangers" as much as we need dedicated team members.

It is amazing how much can be done if we are willing to contribute to the overall good of the project. We go to do what the mission, missionary, or national convention needs. However, preconceived ideas of how things should be done may not actually be the best. The "American" way may not be God's way overseas.

Short-term service can bring out both the best and the worst in us. One grumbling, complaining volunteer can disrupt the unity and effectiveness of a dedicated team. It is important to remember that the best-laid plans will change as schedules are rearranged and unforeseen needs are addressed on the field. The grace of encouraging each other as we do God's work overseas can energize and inspire us even when things go wrong. In a real sense, we belong not only to God, but also to each other. Our talents and gifts are joined together as an offering to God and His global purposes.

Day 3

Serve with Inner Strength

John 15:1-16

I am the vine, you are the branches; he who abides in Me and I in him, he bears much fruit, for apart from Me you can do nothing.
—John 15:5

Have you ever tried to blow up a balloon until you were almost dizzy? Sometimes fear of the unknown can make us feel rather uneasy and dizzy. We may never have done the things we are expected to do now and may never have been in such a different setting.

We need a sense of worth, competency, and acceptance if we are to do our jobs overseas. All the skills in the world, unless permeated with the presence of God's Spirit, will not bring victories.

While you may plan to do God's work and certainly desire to

be fruitful, a volunteer who draws from his or her own strength will wither like a branch severed from a tree. The following truths will determine whether your work will succeed or fail:

1. Cleansing by God from all known sin.

2. Abiding in the power and presence of Christ.

3. Working in the spirit of love.

4. Keeping the commandments of Christ.

5. Knowing God has chosen you to bear fruit.

6. Asking the Father to bless the mission and honor His name.

The strength of a Christ-centered life will energize you, and you can say with Isaiah, *Those who wait for the LORD will gain new strength; they will mount up with wings like eagles, they will run and not get tired, they will walk and not become weary* (Isaiah 40:31). This is the purpose of our thirty-day devotional – to assist each of us to serve with inner strength.

Day 4

Serve with Urgency

John 9:1-7

We must work the works of Him who sent Me as long as it is day; night is coming when no one can work. —John 9:4

Although Jesus was interested in correct belief, He was far more concerned about correct actions. He felt compelled to come to earth to seek and save humanity from sin. He felt the need to go through Samaria and witness to a sinful woman who desperately needed the living water. He steadfastly set His face toward Jerusalem, knowing it meant rejection and certain death.

Jesus saw a blind man and strongly stated to His disciples, *We must work the works of Him who sent Me as long as it is day; night is coming when no one can work.* He knew that healing this man on the Sabbath would bring opposition from the religious leaders, but He understood that opportunities for doing good do not last forever. The "take it or leave it" attitude, this idea that we are only obedient when it is convenient, is not acceptable to God.

Jesus gives us the definition of "day" by saying, *While I am in the world, I am the Light of the world* (John 9:5). A day was the time of Jesus' earthly ministry. His time on earth only lasted thirty-three years, and everything He needed to accomplish had already been settled by God, the Father. He did not have time to debate theological issues, but with a sense of urgency, He served others. Jesus' time on earth may be over, but His work continues through those who have repented and believed in Him.

Matthew 5:14 tells us that we are the light of the world. As long as we have breath in our lungs, then we are able to serve with urgency. However, there will be a day when Christ will come, and again the light will be removed from this world; the night is coming and there is work to do. This mission trip is your chance to do some of God's work while there is still daylight.

It is not enough just to say, "I'll go!" You must prepare for the task you are expected to do. You must open your eyes to every opportunity. The day of service is before you, but the night is coming. The blind of heart are waiting. Like Jesus, we must work now, for we may never have this opportunity again.

Day 5

The Power to Serve

Acts 1:1-12

> But you will receive power when the Holy Spirit
> has come upon you; and you shall be My witnesses
> both in Jerusalem, and in all Judea and Samaria,
> and even to the remotest part of the earth.
> —Acts 1:8

Christians need to understand that eternal victories do not occur apart from the power of the Holy Spirit. Energy is wasted because Christians do not claim the power of God to do the task. In witnessing, we attempt to lead people to repentance and new life. How foolish to think that we can do these things apart from God! Acts 1:8 says, *You will receive power when the Holy Spirit has come upon you.* It is not our strength, ability, college degrees, or any other earthly achievement that brings transformation in someone's life. However, God, through His Spirit, dwells within us, and He will use us to accomplish His work in the lives of others.

You must understand that God has chosen you for the purpose of witnessing. John 15:16 says, *You did not choose Me but I chose you, and appointed you that you would go and bear fruit.* These verses should give you confidence to go out into the highways and byways and proclaim the gospel. God has chosen you and created a purpose within you to bring forth fruit as a witness. Embrace this truth and recognize the power of God that lives within you.

The Holy Spirit must be recognized in your life. To the early followers of Jesus, the Holy Spirit came with power and signs that empowered them to do the task God had given them to do. Today, the Holy Spirit still empowers us to accomplish what He calls us to do. The Holy Spirit is in our lives, and as we surrender willfully to Him, we will feel that power from within. When sin is removed from our lives, the Holy Spirit can accomplish His purpose in us.

A powerful witness is the result of surrendering to the Holy Spirit. Acts 1:8 explains where we should go to witness: *even to the remotest part of the earth.* This places no limit on our witness for Christ. Today's Christians who are led by the Holy Spirit will want to witness to the world with boldness, wisdom, and power as the early Christians did. God is leading you on this project, and He will empower you through the Holy Spirit to accomplish His task.

Day 6

Acting Like Who You Are

Galatians 5:22-26

But the fruit of the Spirit is love, joy, peace, patience, kindness, goodness, faithfulness, gentleness, self-control; against such things there is no law. Now those who belong to Christ Jesus have crucified the flesh with its passions and desires. If we live by the Spirit, let us also walk by the Spirit. Let us not become boastful, challenging one another, envying one another.
—Galatians 5:22-26

Who is she? Can you tell by the way she dresses and talks or by the way she acts? Who is he? Can you tell by his conversation or by the way he relates to others? The adage "Actions speak louder than words" takes on new meaning as you serve in another culture.

Church leaders in one Caribbean country cautioned a team of volunteers from the United States: "When you walk down the street, do not dress and act like a tourist. The people of our country expect those who work with us in our churches to reflect Christian dress, actions, and conversation when they are shopping, sightseeing, and ministering in our churches."

Always be aware of the image you portray while volunteering

overseas. Just because something is acceptable in the United States does not mean it is acceptable in a foreign culture.

Day 7

God's Love Breaks Through Barriers

John 4:5-42

Jesus answered and said to her, "Everyone who drinks of this water will thirst again; but whoever drinks of the water that I shall give him shall never thirst; but the water that I will give him will become in him a well of water springing up to eternal life."
—John 4:13-14

There are many reasons why you might fail as a short-term volunteer. Even missionaries who learn the language and show sensitivity to cultural differences never fully become assimilated in a foreign culture. How, then, can we expect inexperienced volunteers to accomplish anything useful and eternal in a few days when so many barriers exist? Language, racial differences, economic barriers, different political systems, and different family customs are possible barriers to the task.

You go ready to help, love, give, share, accept, laugh, and serve. You go ready to do things differently, to smile, and to cry. And what happens? Friendships are formed. Common concerns are expressed. Common frailties are confessed. Common joys are shared. Common problems are discussed. A common

Savior is victoriously proclaimed, and the barriers are forgotten. Christ's love bonds you together as one. This is the miracle you can experience as a volunteer.

Day 8

Prayer Is the Key

Luke 18:1

Now He was telling them a parable to show that at all times they ought to pray and not to lose heart.
—Luke 18:1

Prayer is the key to what happens not only during our mission trip, but also in our becoming prepared spiritually for our service. Jesus teaches extensively about prayer and also practiced it regularly. One would think that Jesus would not need to pray since He was the perfect Son of God, yet He did. We must never use the excuse that we are too busy to pray. The opposite should be the rule. The more we have to do, the more we need to stop and begin the day with prayer. You see God's will revealed through prayer.

When a person prays with all sin repented of, great things happen. Elijah prayed, and as a judgment on the nation, it did not rain for three and a half years (James 5:17). Hannah prayed for a child, and God granted her request (1 Samuel 1:27). Elijah prayed on Mount Carmel to ask God to send fire to prove who was the true God, and the fire fell and consumed not only the sacrifice, but also the wood, the stones, the dust, and the water in the trench (1 Kings 18:37-38). The early church prayed for Peter, who had been arrested, and God miraculously brought Peter out of a very secure prison (Acts 12:1-17). I could mention a lot more, but we all know that there is power in prayer.

Some reasons or causes for failure in prayer are disobedience to God, secret sin, indifference, neglect of mercy, stubbornness, instability, and self-indulgence. God wants to answer us and wants to empower us to do His will, so His Word gives us a guide.

1. Pray from an attitude of humility as you seek God's face (2 Chronicles 7:14).

2. Pray with a complete or wholehearted spirit (Jeremiah 29:13).

3. Pray in faith (Mark 11:24).

4. Pray from a righteous life (James 5:16).

5. Pray in obedience and by being obedient to God (1 John 3:22).

I challenge you to spend some extra time today praying for the potential ministry that God is going to do through your mission trip. God wants to answer any prayer that brings Him glory.

Day 9

Wait for the Power

Acts 1:4-14

Gathering them together, He commanded them not to leave Jerusalem, but to wait for what the Father had promised.
—Acts 1:4

Jesus instructed His disciples to wait in Jerusalem until the power came. The reason this devotional is for thirty days and is to be done just prior to your trip is so that each person can spend time in prayer and supplication for and with one another. We each need time for God to speak to our hearts and for sin to be confessed.

We need to be filled with the Holy Spirit. This filling and control of the Holy Spirit is not just a one-time event. Ephesians 5:18 states that we must be continually filled on a continuous basis. This verse portrays the idea of one putting a container under a faucet and keeping it there, even when it becomes full. In the same manner, each of us must keep our hearts under the "faucet" of God's grace, love, and conviction so that our vessel will always be full of God by His Holy Spirit, leaving no room for self or any other things.

Jesus told the disciples to spend time getting their hearts and attitudes right. They were to spend time together in prayer until they were one. While it may not be possible for you to physically pray together before your trip, you can come together and be one spiritually as you each are working through the daily devotional. Each day your team should be studying the same

Bible verses and reading the same thoughts. The oneness will develop as you daily spend time praying for one another and for the mission God has called you to do. Then when you are physically in the same place, that oneness will grow even deeper.

Today we begin to pray for each other by name. Pray that each person will be sensitive to God as He works on each of you to prepare you. May each person yield to God's influence so that you will receive the same promise Jesus gave to the disciples: *You will receive power when the Holy Spirit has come upon you; and you shall be My witnesses* (Acts 1:8).

Oh, may it happen to us, and may the people we encounter know that we have spent time with Jesus by the presence of His Holy Spirit in all that takes place during our time there. May we see a great multitude come to Christ as happened on the day of Pentecost.

Day 10

Some Amazing Promises

John 14:8-14

Truly, truly, I say to you, he who believes in Me, the works that I do, he will do also; and greater works than these he will do; because I go to the Father.
—John 14:12

In our text today, Philip wanted something from Jesus. Philip said, "Lord, just show us God the Father, and if you do, that will be all we need."

Jesus' reply must have come from a broken heart. He said, "Philip, if you want to know God, just look at Me. I do not do anything of or in My own power. It is God who does the work."

This is an important lesson for each of us. We can do nothing in our own power and strength. If anything happens on our mission trip, it will happen only because we have allowed God to use us. It will be because we have gotten ourselves off the throne of our lives and have allowed Christ to sit on the throne of our hearts as absolute ruler. This is hard, and it is a daily, sometimes a moment-by-moment, process.

Jesus then tells Philip a startling statement in verse 12. This statement is for us as well. He says to us individually, "If you believe in Me, the work that I do you will do as well." Can you imagine that we may do the same works that Jesus did? That promise is astounding! To think that we can do what Jesus did is incredible, but then He says something that seems completely beyond reality. He says, "Philip, not only will you do what I do, but you will do even greater works than I did." Wow! Think of that – doing greater works than Jesus did! How can this be? Can we have more power than Jesus? No, I do not think we can. I think He means greater in extent.

Because of the indwelling of the Holy Spirit in all believers, more can and will be done because His power (the Holy Spirit) is in the lives of all believers everywhere at the same time. While here, Jesus chose to limit Himself to be in only one human body. He chose to limit Himself and could not be everywhere at the same time, but with the coming of the Holy Spirit, all believers around the world can do the same works as Christ did all at the same time; thus, greater works will be done. Whatever it is, home visits and services or physical work, we will be doing greater works. So in a real sense, greater works are being done because of the presence of the Holy Spirit in each of our lives and His going ahead of each of us to prepare the way.

Jesus said in John 14:13, *Whatever you ask in My name, that will I do, so that the Father may be glorified in the Son.* Meditate on this truth today, as well as on the same and greater works. Pray and imagine what God wants to happen on your mission trip as you relax and shop. Begin now asking God to do things through you that will glorify Him. Pray that even the works that Jesus did will be done through you. Pray also for the greater works that will be done through your team members individually and also as a group as you work together.

Day 11

Spiritual Renewal for Service #1

Psalm 51

For I know my transgressions, and my sin is ever
before me.
—Psalm 51:3

As you prepare yourself for your upcoming mission trip, it
is important for you to examine yourself and your relationship to God. If there is any sin, known or unknown, that may
keep you from being spiritually ready for service, you need to
deal with it. A good place to begin is with this chapter in the
Psalms. You will be looking at this psalm for a couple of days
as you prepare for service.

After you have read all of Psalm 51, please return to verse
3 and carefully read it again and see how it applies to spiritual
renewal for service. As David became aware of his sins, he first
acknowledged that he had sinned. Sometimes we may want to
overlook our sin and say, "Well, this is not as bad as what [you
know who] does." The problem is that if we do that, we are
comparing ourselves with someone else instead of with God
and His standard. David was honest and said, *I know my transgressions, and my sin is ever before me.* You need to be honest
with God and with yourself and own up to anything in your
life that is contrary to God, His Word, or your ability to be a
good vessel that He can use on your mission trip.

Some of the obvious sins such as lying, stealing, and lusting
may not be a part of your lifestyle, but pride and selfishness
are constant hindrances to a full commitment to Christ. M.

Baxter rightly said, "Self is always ready to extract its rights as regards honor, comfort, conveniences, property, etc., and self has generally a somewhat magnified view of what its rights are." We need to acknowledge the fact that self and pride often have too much power in our lives.

We must be disciplined Christians to see the sin within our lives. As we draw closer to God, we do not see our righteousness, but our weaknesses. We are most blessed when we develop the ability to see the sin within our lives. It is then that we have something to share with others. Today, begin first of all to examine and identify what is there that should not be, and then acknowledge that it is sin; ask God to deal with it.

Day 12

Spiritual Renewal for Service #2

Psalm 51

For You do not delight in sacrifice, otherwise I would give it; You are not pleased with burnt offering. The sacrifices of God are a broken spirit; a broken and a contrite heart, O God, You will not despise.
—Psalm 51:16-17

We are still looking at Psalm 51 as you are learning how to prepare yourself spiritually for your time of service. Your ministry overseas will be demanding. People will be looking at your life as an example of Christianity. You will want to be ready spiritually. Another way for this to happen is for you not only to acknowledge your sins, but also to confess them to a forgiving God.

First acknowledge that you have sinned and that your sin is really a sin against God. Read all of Psalm 51 and then come back to verses 16-17 and study what God wants from you as you approach Him in confession. Look at the definitions of the words *broken* and *contrite* and apply them to this text concerning where you need to be as you come confessing.

Read Psalm 51 again and notice what David said and how he pleaded with God to forgive him. Note the verses and meditate upon each verse that is a confession verse or in which David seeks for God to cleanse him (look especially at verses 1-2, 7-12, 14). As you read and meditate on these verses, use them as a prayer and pray them back to God for yourself.

After you have spent time with God concerning your confession, reread the Psalm and find the verses that tell what David will be and what he will do after he had been cleansed (see verses 7-8, 10, 12-15, 19). Ask God to do the same in you as He did in David so that you will also be able to follow David's example in verses 13 and 15.

Day 13

Choose to Trust

Nehemiah 4:1

Now it came about that when Sanballat heard that
we were rebuilding the wall, he became furious
and very angry and mocked the Jews.
—Nehemiah 4:1

I t should not surprise us that evil people get angry when their
plans to hinder God's people do not succeed. As Sanballat and
his cronies ridiculed the Jews' construction efforts, Nehemiah
prayed (Nehemiah 4:4-5) and kept building the wall. What you
do right after you pray reveals what you truly believe about God.
A word from God followed by faithful action demonstrates
trust in God, and Nehemiah clearly trusted God: *So we built
the wall* (v. 6).

The opposition escalated, this time with a conspiracy to
fight against Jerusalem and to cause a disturbance in it (v. 8).
What was Nehemiah's response? *We prayed to our God* (v. 9).
Still obstructions came, and still the construction continued.

Opposition to God's work is inevitable. God's enemies
are threatened by the growth of His kingdom, so they move
swiftly and rigorously to stop it. Expect ridicule, injustice, and
even threats when you labor for the Lord, but know that you
are laboring with Him at your side, so turn to Him in prayer
as you work.

Despite the circumstances that we may encounter, we will
choose whether to trust in God or to be fearful. Our enemy,
Satan, will try to get us to be fearful and to retreat from sharing

or speaking out for God. We will choose whether we will trust God and speak boldly or if we will listen to the enemy and remain silent. Follow Nehemiah's example; choose to trust.

Day 14

Our Real Enemy

Ephesians 6:10-12

Finally, be strong in the Lord and in the strength of His might. Put on the full armor of God, so that you will be able to stand firm against the schemes of the devil. For our struggle is not against flesh and blood, but against the rulers, against the powers, against the world forces of this darkness, against the spiritual forces of wickedness in the heavenly places.
—Ephesians 6:10-12

Today will begin a five-day study from Ephesians 6 about our enemy and the spiritual weapons we need to combat this foe. Today we look at our foe.

Paul was fully aware that there is an enemy to the cause of Christ. It is not the Roman Catholic Church, the Jehovah's Witnesses, or social issues. These are only symptoms of our true enemy: Satan. Paul describes our enemy. As we look at these descriptions, let us be mindful of Satan's tactics so that we do not fall prey to his schemes.

Paul says that Satan is "wily," or deceitful. Second Thessalonians 2 and Revelation 12:9 both talk about Satan deceiving the whole earth. Satan is a liar who seeks to destroy and confuse us using his deceitfulness. He will use any and all means to cause us to stumble or to take our eyes off Christ. In 2 Corinthians 11:14, we read that Satan will even transform himself into an angel of light. We need to be on our guard so that we will not be deceived to turn away from an intimate walk with Christ. If Satan can get us to take our eyes off Christ, then we will be defeated. If he can get us to be impatient with one another, have hard feelings toward one another, or even toward those we encounter, then we will be defeated and Satan will rejoice.

Peter tells us in 1 Peter 5:8 that our enemy is like a roaring lion walking around seeking someone to devour. Oh, may we not be his next prey! During this time of devotion and also during your time together on your mission trip, I want you to always remember: *Greater is He who is in you than he who is in the world* (1 John 4:4).

May we realize today that Satan will seek to hinder any work that we attempt for Christ. Let us be prepared for his attack and pray for victory over every temptation and attack that he will throw against us. Pray for each other to be strong in the Lord as Satan comes prowling.

Spiritual Weapons #1

Ephesians 6:10-18

Stand firm therefore, having girded your loins
with truth, and having put on the breastplate of
righteousness, and having shod your feet with the
preparation of the gospel of peace.
—Ephesians 6:14-15

Today we begin to look at our spiritual weapons. As we saw yesterday, Satan is actively seeking to devour unsuspecting individuals. We see that he (the thief) comes only to kill, steal, and destroy, but Jesus comes to bring life, and that more abundantly (John 10:10). If we are to have abundant life and not be a victim of Satan, we need to be clothed with the whole armor of God. Paul says that the whole armor is needed to be able to withstand these attacks (Ephesians 6:13).

Picture yourself as the soldier who is being equipped. We are to take our stand against Satan by having a belt of truth. Truth is what holds together all other items of our warfare and makes them effective. The belt on a Roman soldier held his tunic tight so that he might be free in his movement. The belt also provided a place for his sword to hang. Truth is so essential; Satan is a liar, and he has deceived and fed his lies to the people we will encounter. We are to be people who not only tell the truth but also exhibit truthfulness. If we are not truthful, then everything else and all of our other weapons will be in jeopardy.

In the same verse and probably in the same breath, Paul tells us to be equipped with a breastplate of righteousness. The breastplate guarded the most vital parts of the body – the heart, lungs, stomach, and other vital organs. We need to have our hearts covered with righteousness so that they remain impregnable to Satan's attacks.

Because of what Jesus did on the cross, God has imputed righteousness to us. This means that God looks at us as though we are without sin. This imputed righteousness is ours by our faithful and obedient response of asking Christ to save us. Because of Christ dwelling within us by the power of the Holy Spirit, our passions are redirected. The drives and instincts of our lives move under the power of the indwelling Christ. Each of us must allow our emotions to be covered by the righteousness of God. If we have on the breastplate of righteousness, Satan cannot get to those vital organs that have so much control in our lives. If we are not covered by the breastplate, we will be moved and controlled by Satan.

Next is to have our feet covered with the preparation of the gospel of peace. As we are on a mission, we will be doing a lot of walking. It will be important for us to have good walking shoes so we will have sure footing and also so our feet will not suffer from the long walks. We will be walking through areas where the enemy has thrown stumbling blocks. We must be ready and be prepared to share the gospel of peace in these areas where Satan has had such a stronghold. Isaiah 52:7 says that those who bring the good news of peace have beautiful feet.

You might look at your feet or some of the feet of your team members and laugh at the thought of those feet being beautiful. However, even if you have knobby toes, God sees beautiful toes because you are sharing His good news. We each must have a missionary spirit, an evangelical zeal, and a heart prepared to carry the gospel everywhere. Here again we must remember Zechariah 4:6: *"Not by might nor by power, but by My Spirit,"* *says the LORD of hosts.*

God is the only one who can empower us to be effective witnesses. Examine yourself today and see if you have these three pieces of the soldier's armor. If you do not have them, ask God to clothe you with them.

Day 16

Spiritual Weapons # 2

Ephesians 6:10-18

In addition to all, taking up the shield of faith with which you will be able to extinguish all the flaming arrows of the evil one.
—Ephesians 6:16

Yesterday we began putting on our spiritual armor to withstand the wiles of Satan. We looked at the belt of truth, the breastplate of righteousness, and the shoes of the gospel of peace. Today we look at one more of the pieces that we all need continually. Paul tells us in verse 16, *In addition to all, taking up the shield of faith.* We are told that above all things, we need a shield of faith.

Faith is so very important for each of us. Hebrews 11 tells us how important faith is for us. In fact, the writer of Hebrews says that if we do not have faith, we cannot please God. To many people, having faith seems foolish. The idea of putting one's faith in something that cannot be seen, such as God, is utter nonsense to them. But we of the household of faith understand how important it is. Yet do we really practice it completely? Hebrews 11:1 says that *faith is the assurance of things hoped for.* In other words, faith believes that something will take place even before we see it become visual.

As we pray for individuals each day and for God's glory, and as we sense God's voice and leading for the salvation of a person or a particular event, we should believe and act as if what we have prayed for is already a reality. Read the entire eleventh chapter of Hebrews and see how individuals exhibited faith in the promises of the Lord. Each of these individuals trusted (believed) that what God said was a reality, and they acted in obedience.

Take Noah for an example. Read Hebrews 11:7. God told Noah that He was going to destroy the world by a flood of water. Up until the flood occurred, it had never even rained. The earth was like a ball in a terrarium. The heat caused things to be moisturized so that dew came upon the plants; no rain was needed. However, God came to Noah and said, "Build a boat because I am going to make it rain until even the mountains are covered with water." I can almost hear Noah saying to God, "Okay, God, but I have a question. What is a boat, and what is rain?"

The Bible says that Noah acted in faith, moved with reverent fear, and prepared the ark. Can you imagine the neighbors constantly coming over to where Noah and his sons were constructing the ark? Whenever Noah told them what he was doing and why, I am sure they laughed and told him he was crazy. I have experienced that same kind of reaction during previous trips. While in Russia, my interpreter and I told some people about Christ and told them that Jesus was coming soon to judge the world. They told us that was foolish. Some people have laughed at our attempts. However, we believed what God had commanded, to "go and tell," and we were obedient in spite of what was said to us.

In the book of Ephesians, Paul says that having faith is like having a shield to ward off the fiery darts of Satan. The Roman soldier used his shield as a means of protection. We also must use our faith as a shield. Satan will throw his fiery darts at us to wound us and to belittle us. We must make use of our faith in God to give us strength, and then go on in spite of any opposition. When abuse comes, when insults come, or when we are rejected, we must exercise faith and allow that to protect us and to stir us on until we have finished what God has directed us to do.

This kind of faith is not in our own ability or in anyone else's. This faith is only in God and in His faithfulness to accomplish what He has said. Today I ask you: Do you have faith? Do you believe that God will do something great even though it has not yet happened? Has God been speaking to you about what He wants to do through you? Will you act upon that word and even see it as a reality now before it actually comes to pass? James 2:14-26 reminds us that if we say we believe something, then we need to act upon it and not just talk about it.

Today I pray that God will give you a word about this trip. When it comes, believe that it will take place, and step out in that assurance even now.

Spiritual Weapons # 3

Ephesians 6:10-18

And take the helmet of salvation, and the sword of the Spirit, which is the word of God.
—Ephesians 6:17

We are told that we are to take on the whole armor and not omit any piece. The next piece is the helmet of salvation. Having the knowledge that we are saved is essential. Knowing we are saved is a divine guarantee of God's divine protection and ultimate deliverance. We can live and serve in confidence that the Christian life is secure because salvation has been given by God.

When we put on the helmet, we are safe in the sense of being delivered from the destructive powers of evil forces, but also that we have the confidence that nothing, absolutely nothing, can separate us from the love of God. If God is for us, it does not matter who is against us. If we have the helmet of salvation, we can live boldly even in the face of persecution and under the threat of death. Having the knowledge that we are Christ's can enable us, like Paul, to say, *I say, and prefer rather to be absent from the body and to be at home with the Lord* (2 Corinthians 5:8). We can know and trust God no matter what the enemy may throw at us. Read Romans 8:31-39 and claim the victory that is ours in Christ.

Not only are we to have a sure knowledge that we are saved in Christ throughout all eternity, but we are to have the sword of the Spirit – the Word of God. It is important that we have and are skilled in handling the sword of the Spirit. Hebrews 4:12 tells us how powerful the Word of God is. Please read that verse and meditate upon it.

Not only must we have the sword of the Spirit, but we must also know how to handle the sword skillfully. Therefore, we must practice on a regular basis. The more we practice with the sword, the more skillful we will become. Having a sword without ever taking it out of the scabbard is foolish. How can people truly be saved if they do not use the Word of God? Please read Romans 10:17 to be reminded of a great truth. We must each practice using our sword on a regular basis, but remember that it is *the sword of the Spirit*. God's Spirit is what brings conviction and salvation.

Thank God today for the helmet of salvation and the sword of the Spirit. Grasp the awesome truth of our position in Christ. Pray that God will give each of you opportunities to use your sword today and also on your mission trip.

Spiritual Weapons #4

Ephesians 6:10-20

With all prayer and petition pray at all times in the Spirit, and with this in view, be on the alert with all perseverance and petition for all the saints, and pray on my behalf, that utterance may be given to me in the opening of my mouth, to make known with boldness the mystery of the gospel, for which I am an ambassador in chains; that in proclaiming it I may speak boldly, as I ought to speak.
—Ephesians 6:18-20

Today I have included two more verses in our reading. I hope that the reading and rereading of the same text has caused you to understand the seriousness of putting on the whole armor. We must realize that we have an enemy, and because of that, we must always be praying in the Spirit. This is what Ephesians 6:18-20 tells us. All the armor will be of no avail in the Christian battles without the dynamic power that comes in this way; to be watchful in the Spirit is to stay alive and to be alert.

Paul says that the final piece of armor is prayer. To truly combat Satan and be victorious, we need to be continually in prayer and to pray *in the Spirit*. I think this means that the Holy Spirit guides and directs our prayers. As we pray, we are to be sensitive to the Holy Spirit's voice.

For example, a few years ago, when my uncle was in Russia, Irina, his interpreter, was praying about their transportation back to Bryansk from Novozybkov. She sensed that they were to go in the van with the driver they had had all week. At first it seemed as if it was not going to happen because of his rates, but just before they needed to buy the train tickets, their driver called Irina and said that some other person needed to go to Bryansk, and he offered to take them at a reduced rate. Praise the Lord that Irina was sensitive to the Holy Spirit's leading and did not buy the train tickets at first.

Paul says to always pray and also to be constantly watchful in the Spirit with all perseverance. Jesus tells us to be watchful or alert because we do not know when Jesus will return (Mark 13:33). We are told in Luke to be watchful and alert to escape the things that are coming and to be able to stand before Christ when He comes (Luke 21:33-36). It is crucial that we pray for ourselves and for other believers that each of us will be alert and sensitive to God's voice.

We need to pray for one another that we each will speak with boldness to make known the mystery of the gospel. For we, like Paul, are *ambassadors for Christ* (2 Corinthians 5:20), and therefore we must speak boldly. When ambassadors speak or take a stand, they are doing so with the power of the country that they represent. During the time of the Romans, a region occupied by the Roman government sent an ambassador with a small delegation to the border of the country and waited for an approaching army. When the opposing army came, the general in charge came and stood before the Roman ambassador. The ambassador drew a line in the ground and said, "Imperial Rome says you are not to cross this line." The general thought for a moment and then commanded his troops to return the way they had come. The enemy general knew that he could easily kill this small delegation, but he also knew that the power of the whole Roman Empire was behind this one man, for he represented Rome and all its might.

We need to realize that when we speak the gospel message,

we have the power of the whole Godhead behind us. We do not speak and must not speak in our own strength, but in the power and might of the King of kings and Lord of lords. Today, thank God for His power. God Himself is behind us, and His power rests in us by the indwelling of His Holy Spirit.

Day 19

Revive Us Again

Psalm 85

Restore us, O God of our salvation, and cause Your indignation toward us to cease. Will You be angry with us forever? Will You prolong Your anger to all generations? Will You not Yourself revive us again, that Your people may rejoice in You?
—Psalm 85:4-6

A favorite hymn written by William Mackay in 1863 has these words:

> Revive us again, fill each heart with Thy love;
>   May each soul be rekindled with fire from above.
> Hallelujah! Thine the glory, hallelujah! Amen!
>   Hallelujah! Thine the glory, revive us again.

Life has a way of dragging us down. Praise, at times, often slides into mere empty sentences, and our hallelujahs just become boring words. The race that we are running may have simply become a rat race. We long to breathe the fresh wind of the Spirit of God in our lives. We all need revival. This fact is true for every one of you on the mission team and all whom you will encounter.

As you minister on your mission trip, you cannot and will not lead people to experience revival if you have not experienced it yourself. The road to revival is not unlike your initial path to the Lord. It is a road of repentance and faith that leads to the flowing fountain of gratitude. Read Colossians 2:6-7 and see that we are to continue to live in Christ and be strengthened in the faith to be *overflowing with gratitude.*

What freshness will come to our relationship with God as we daily seek His forgiveness and leadership! As the psalmist describes it, *Lovingkindness and truth have met together; righteousness and peace have kissed each other. Truth springs from the earth, and righteousness looks down from heaven* (Psalm 85:10-11). Yes, the Lord will give that which is good.

It is God's desire for us to live in such a way that our lives reflect His presence and power. Jesus puts it this way in John 10:10: *The thief comes only to steal and kill and destroy; I came that they may have life, and have it abundantly.* We must be disciplined Christians. As we draw closer to God, we should not see our own righteousness, but our own weakness. We are most blessed when we develop the ability to see our need to be more like Christ and our need for an abundant life.

Your ministry on your mission trip will be demanding. People will be looking at your lives as examples of what Christianity really is. You will want to be at your very best. Pray that each of your lives will be an example of the joy of the Lord and the fullness of His Holy Spirit.

The Joys of Yielding to God's Conviction

Psalm 32

I acknowledged my sin to You, and my iniquity I did
not hide; I said, "I will confess my transgressions to
the LORD"; and You forgave the guilt of my sin.
—Psalm 32:5

Today we look at the joy that is ours when we respond to the
convicting power of God upon our lives. We also see the
effects that unconfessed sins have on us. When God brings
conviction upon us, it is His desire for us to quickly respond to
Him and do what is needed and what He leads us to do. When
we have our sins forgiven, our sins are covered and we are
blessed. We see that God is our hiding place and the one who
preserves us from trouble. He is also the one who surrounds
us with songs that we sing because of our deliverance brought
about by His mighty hand.

If we do not respond to the prompting, then we will have
to be treated as horses or mules that must have a bit and bridle
so that they will be directed to go the proper way (Psalm 32:9).
God wants to instruct us and teach us in the way that we are
to go. Our text says that He even wants to counsel us with His
eye upon us (Psalm 32:8). We can be glad in the Lord and even
shout for joy when we are upright in heart. Spend some time
today rejoicing in the Lord. Thank Him for His love and for
His working in your lives. Thank Him that He loves us so much
that He brings conviction into our lives when we have sinned.

His conviction is a sign of His love for us. When He brings

conviction upon us and we do not immediately respond, the psalmist shares the effects it has upon us. He says that when God convicts us and we do not respond, our grief becomes so intense that it drains our strength and destroys our vital energy (Psalm 32:4). It becomes like a fire in our bones. While we try to smother our sin, it rages within. The effects of the guilt will drive us to sorrow.

The psalmist says that God's hand was heavy upon him (v. 4). God's hand is very helpful when it uplifts, but it is dreadfully painful when it presses down. The psalmist tells us that the energy of our souls becomes dry and our body will seem to be short of the needed fluids to sustain it. But when we confess our sins to God, we find forgiveness, and life is once again restored to us. If there is any unconfessed sin in your life today, respond to God's convicting power and quickly acknowledge it so that the joy of the Lord will be full in your life again.

Christian Depression

1 Kings 19:1-18

And he was afraid and arose and ran for his life
and came to Beersheba, which belongs to Judah,
and left his servant there. But he himself went a
day's journey into the wilderness, and came and
sat down under a juniper tree; and he requested for
himself that he might die, and said, "It is enough;
now, O LORD, take my life, for I am not better than
my fathers."
—1 Kings 19:3-4

Christian workers often pass through periods of depression.
Passing through the experience itself may not be detrimen-
tal, but remaining that way for a period of time can adversely
affect your Christian ministry. Depression can come even after a
victory with God. A mountaintop experience with God is often
followed by a valley of despair. Elijah certainly experienced this.

Physical fatigue can also lead to depression. It is important
for a Christian witness to be physically, as well as spiritually,
strong. As a volunteer overseas, you must be alert to physical
fatigue. You need adequate rest in order to witness effectively,
for even Christian zeal and enthusiasm cannot endure when
you are overcome by physical fatigue.

Depression increases when you are alone. This is shown in
Elijah's life when he was alone under a juniper tree and later
alone in a cave. It was then that his depression became greatest. It is important that you remain a part of a group and share

with them not only the victories that have happened in your life, but also the sorrows and struggles you face. God is able to deliver you from your depression and bring you ultimate victory, or He might be using it to draw you closer to Him. James 1:3 reminds us that *the testing of your faith produces endurance.* Your battle with depression may be for a season, or it may be a lifelong struggle. One thing we can be certain of is that God is in control and He knows what He is doing. In the case of Elijah, God revealed His presence to Elijah and reminded him of his purpose and calling.

The most common time for homesickness and depression during a short-term mission trip is midweek. The emotional energy present upon arrival has been depleted, and lack of proper rest and the different situations have taken their toll. There have been victories for God Sunday through Tuesday, but there is often a letdown on Wednesday. Fortunately, you will pass through this period. So watch for signs of depression during your overseas experience. Draw close to God through Bible study and prayer. He can and will bring triumph over depression.

A Daily Struggle

Romans 8:1-15

For the mind set on the flesh is death, but the mind set on the Spirit is life and peace, because the mind set on the flesh is hostile toward God; for it does not subject itself to the law of God, for it is not even able to do so, and those who are in the flesh cannot please God.

—Romans 8:6-8

I do not know about you, but every day I face a struggle between the indwelling Spirit of God and my old fleshly nature. I do not believe that I am unique in this. Paul struggled with this as well. Read Romans 7:7-25. Paul said that he never got around to doing the good that he wanted to do, but those things that he found himself doing were things that he didn't want to do. Paul cried out, *Wretched man that I am! Who will set me free from the body of this death?* (Romans 7:24). He concluded that delivery is through Jesus Christ (v. 25).

Paul then shared more about this daily struggle between the Spirit and the flesh. Paul said that if our minds are constantly on the things of the flesh, then we are at war with God, for a carnal mind is not and cannot be subject to the laws of God (Romans 8:7). He then said that if we are in the flesh, we cannot please God (v. 8). Those are very strong and powerful words. They are words to make us shudder as we are so very prone to do what the flesh desires.

However, we are not left without hope. Paul said that if we

have Christ in us (and we do if we have repented and confessed our sins to Christ and trusted in Him), then He will make us alive by His Spirit. Earlier, in Romans 5:20-6:23, Paul gave a solution to this daily struggle. In fact, I would encourage you to read all of Romans chapters 5-8. In chapter 6, Paul told us to realize that the *old self* has been buried with Christ in baptism.

Therefore, we are to consider ourselves as dead in regard to sin. How many dead men and women commit adultery? How many dead men and women get drunk? How many dead people commit any type of sin? Knowing that we have died to sin when we accepted Christ and that sin should not have dominion over us is one thing, but living out this truth moment by moment is another matter. It is a struggle that we will have all of our lives.

Some people might struggle with some things that others are not even tempted by – for example, smoking and drinking. Some people used to smoke and drink, but now neither of these things hold any power over them. They may still be struggling daily with some other things, however. What one person may struggle with may not even bother you, for you may have the victory over it. In the same way, the things that are your source of struggle may not be so with your fellow brother or sister in Christ.

I hope that we each can take courage and realize that God is able to get the victory as we yield ourselves more and more to Him in those troubling areas. We can gain the victory. Actually, that is not right. *We* cannot, but Christ can gain the victory in us as we yield these struggles to Him. I encourage each of you to let Christ have control in those areas in which you struggle. Know also that when we do slip into sin, His grace is more abundant than our sin (Romans 5:20).

A Fully Surrendered Life #1

Romans 12:1-4

Therefore I urge you, brethren, by the mercies of God, to present your bodies a living and holy sacrifice, acceptable to God, which is your spiritual service of worship.
—Romans 12:1

Is your life fully surrendered to Christ? In our text, Paul deals with our Christian duty – a fully surrendered life. Paul said that we must demonstrate our commitment to Christ by doing three things: presenting our bodies, refusing to conform to this world, and being transformed through renewed minds. We do all of this because of God's mercy toward us. Mercy can best be described as compassion to us because of helplessness. We were and are helpless, so God demonstrated His love for us by giving us His mercy.

Paul first said that because of God's mercy, we should present our bodies to God as a living sacrifice. The term *present* is the technical expression for presenting a victim for sacrifice. Paul is clearly saying that believers need to hand over their bodies to God in a manner resembling the way the people of Israel presented their offerings to God. The body we are to present is the whole person. We are to give God every part of our bodies – our minds, our emotions, our wills, our sexual natures, our appetites, etc. Paul said that we are not to kill our sacrifice, but are to present it alive unto God. This is the very least that we can do.

Our sacrifice is to be holy and acceptable to God. Please read Romans 8:1-17 for more clarification about a holy body. We can engage in mighty sacrificial acts that, like Cain's sacrifice, are totally unacceptable to God because of the attitude in which they are presented. However, when we yield to the Lord as a means of expressing a living, vital, holy experience, the Lord is as well pleased as He was with the sacrifices of Abel. I ask each of us, "Are we living sacrifices?"

Paul then told us to refuse to conform to this world. Paul was not talking about the physical earth, but the *evil age* (Galatians 1:4) in which we live. We are told to not become like everybody else. The J. B. Phillips translation says, *Don't let the world around you squeeze you into its own mould* (Romans 12:2). As believers, we have the unique privilege and tension-filled opportunity to live in this present world, but we are to live as if we are living in the world to come. It is very tempting to identify with the present world and its culture without thought or question. However, by doing this we become totally indistinguishable from the pagans among whom we live. The temptation and pressure that come to us tempt us to simply fit in, yet a committed life to Jesus Christ is shown by the degree in which the believer stays in the secular world without being trapped by it and without failing to be a witness to it. Jesus said that we are in the world but not of the world. Ask yourself: "Am I or have I allowed this present world to squeeze me into its mold? Am I in the world but not of the world, or am I not only in the world, but also of the world?"

A Fully Surrendered Life #2

Romans 12:1-4

And do not be conformed to this world, but be
transformed by the renewing of your mind, that
you may prove what the will of God is, that which
is good and acceptable and perfect.
—Romans 12:2

Today we conclude the study on a fully surrendered life that
we began yesterday. We talked about presenting ourselves
as living sacrifices and refusing to be conformed to this world.
Now we look at the third aspect. A fully surrendered Christian
is one whose life is transformed by the renewing of the mind.

The word *transformed* is an interesting word. It is the same
word that is used to describe Jesus when He was on the Mount
of Transfiguration when the pent-up glory of heaven suddenly
burned through the confines of His earthly body. The word is
metamorphosis. It is the same word that is used to describe what
happens to a caterpillar that changes into a butterfly. In both
of these cases, there was a change that began on the inside. The
Christian is to be someone who is so changed on the inside that
everything is different even on the outside. A caterpillar before
could only creep along, but as a butterfly, it now can soar and
travel to new heights and experience what was not possible as
a caterpillar. The same is true for the Christian. We are able
to soar to great heights and experience what never would have
been possible prior to coming to Christ.

The metamorphosis comes through the renewing of our

minds. We renew our minds as we take on the mind of Christ. Look at and meditate on Philippians 2:5-13. In this passage we are instructed to have the mind, or attitude, of Christ. Christ did not cling to His divinity and place of privilege as the Son of God, but became like a man and was obedient even to the point of death (Philippians 2:8).

Jesus could have said, "I do not want to be a man. I do not want to become contaminated by even touching them, let alone becoming one of them." Yet He came and became a man in obedience to His heavenly Father. We also must be willing to associate with those less desirable who need Christ. We are not to join in the sinful things that they may be doing, though. Jesus was in a man's body, but He never sinned. We also must be willing to be with "sinners" without participating in the sins they commit.

The real temptation for Christians is to think they are better than others, and therefore should not even associate with those who do not know Christ. We are warned about that in Romans 12:3. We must not get haughty and have an air of superiority about us. We need to realize that if it were not for the grace of God, we also could be doing what those individuals are doing.

Today I ask each one of you: "Are you a fully surrendered Christian? Are you presenting your body as a living sacrifice? Are you being conformed to Christ or to the world? Are you being changed so completely on the inside that it is changing every part of your life?"

Yes, these are tough questions, but they are questions that we must answer as we prepare ourselves to be used by God.

Love Is Essential

1 Corinthians 13

But now faith, hope, love, abide these three; but the greatest of these is love.
—1 Corinthians 13:13

Paul was writing to the church at Corinth. The church had a multitude of problems, but I think that all the problems had their roots in their lack of real love in what they did and said. We also can fall into the same attitude as the Corinthians. They were busy with their work that was all done without God's love as the motivating factor. How often have we gone out to sing, speak, or give solely out of a sense of duty rather than from a heart overflowing with love for Jesus? How often do we live our lives before others without God's love controlling us?

Real love – the love that comes from God and is the type of love that Christ demonstrated on the cross – is described in these verses. Paul said, *Love is patient, love is kind and is not jealous; love does not brag and is not arrogant, does not act unbecomingly; it does not seek its own, is not provoked, does not take into account a wrong suffered, does not rejoice in unrighteousness, but rejoices with the truth; bears all things, believes all things, hopes all things, endures all things. Love never fails* (1 Corinthians 13:4-8).

We can preach, teach, speak, and sing with the voices of men and of angels, but if we do not have love, we will sound like the noise that is made when one beats on a cymbal or blasts a horn. We can have deep faith and vast knowledge, but if we do not have love, it is worthless. We can see the poor and give them food to eat, and even die as a martyr, but if we do so without love, it does not profit us anything (1 Corinthians 13:1-3). Doing all things in and through love must be our motive and our goal.

Real love is even the test of whether we are really believers. Read 1 John 4:7-21. John said that if a person does not love, he does not know God, for God is love (1 John 4:8). John then said that if a man says he loves God but hates his brother (*brother* is a generic term for fellow man, as well as one's own brother), then that person is a liar (1 John 4:20).

It is so important for each of us to be controlled by and operate each minute in and through His love. We learn to love by the example of God's love for us – as when God sent Jesus to the cross to take away our sin. Pray today for His love to infill you and control you in all that you do.

Day 26

Warnings from Gethsemane

Luke 22:31-34; 39-48; 54-62

When He arrived at the place, He said to them,
"Pray that you may not enter into temptation."
—Luke 22:40

Today I want us to look at some warnings that, if ignored, could hinder your efforts on your mission trip. As you are preparing your heart for your ministry, you need to heed these warnings so that you are not hindered. These three warnings are progressive. The first leads to the second, and the result of the first and second leads to the third.

One of the first warnings is having overconfidence in self. Jesus told Peter that Satan desired to have him so that he could sift him as one does with wheat. Peter was hurt, and he boastfully said that he was ready to go to jail or even die with Jesus. I would encourage you to read each of the gospel accounts of this event (Matthew 26:31-35; Mark 14:27-31; Luke 22:31-44; John 13:31-38).

The Bible indicates that Peter had no idea what was about to happen. He was always so certain about his own ability and power. A big danger is for us to be like Peter and rely on ourselves and our past experiences and to go out and do things in our own strength. If we do, we will utterly fail. It is easy to work in our own power and strength. We can even get so busy doing things for God that we fail to spend time with Him. Please do not fall into this trap of Satan.

We find the second warning in verses 39-48. We are warned not to fail to be in prayer during times of danger. Again, please read the accounts in two of the other gospels (Matthew 26:30, 36-46; Mark 14:26, 32-42). In the other two accounts, we find that three times Jesus found the disciples sleeping when prayer was needed. How often we "fall asleep" during those times when we should be in prayer! When we do fall asleep, we will be overcome with fear and may even lash out as Simon Peter did (John 18:10-11).

Prayerlessness in the face of danger could be disastrous to the team. You may ask, "Are you saying that we will encounter great danger during our ministry?" I do not know for sure, but I do know that when God works, Satan gets upset and stirs up trouble. The solution is for each person to do what Jesus said in Luke 18:1: *At all times they ought to pray and not to lose heart.*

One of our greatest dangers is prayerlessness during this preparation, and especially during our days on the mission field.

The third warning (a direct outcome of what happens when the first and second warnings are ignored) is that of having a broken relationship with Jesus. We see this in verses 54-62. The Bible says in Luke 22:54 that Peter followed Jesus at a distance. When we have overconfidence in our own efforts, we cease to pray. We soon find ourselves in a broken relationship with Jesus and following Him at a great distance. We may even find ourselves denying our Lord like Peter did.

Having a broken relationship with Jesus is a serious matter, but one that can be taken care of. The first step is to be broken by it like Peter was (v. 62). It was not until after the resurrection of Jesus that Peter was finally restored. As with Peter, it takes the presence of the risen Lord in our hearts to completely restore us.

I pray that each of us will heed these warnings from Gethsemane. If we do not heed these warnings, we may be destined to repeat the results of ignoring them.

Availability Plus Christ

John 6:1-14

Therefore when the people saw the sign which
He had performed, they said, "This is truly the
Prophet who is to come into the world."
—John 6:14

Jesus teaches us something very important in this text. Let
us look at the elements of the lesson. First, there is the lad. He
was there when he could have been comfortably at home. He
could have said, "This is my lunch, and I am not going to share
it." However, he came forward and gave all he had to Jesus. I
hope that each of us will be like this boy. I pray that we are willing to give our all. I thank God that you did not decide to stay
in your comfort zone, but you were willing to leave that place
of safety and security to go overseas and give your all to Jesus.

Second, the lad had so little to offer. There were five thousand
men, in addition to women and children. The lad gave all that
he had even though it was so insufficient. Each of us are like
that lad. We don't have much, and the need is so overwhelm-
ing. We may be saying, "I am only one person and there are so
many lost people who need Christ. What can I do or what can
be done with what I have, with my skills and ability?" The key
is not how little we have compared to the great need, but the
key is that we are willing to share and give all that we do have.

Third and most important, there is the Lord. Without Him
there is no story, no miracle, and no multiplication of resources.
With Christ present in any situation, there is the possibility of

the unusual, the unexpected, and the miraculous happening. When the lad gave all that he had to Jesus, something happened. The same will be true for each member of our team and our interpreters. When we give all that we have to Jesus, the possibility of the miraculous is always present.

In this story, more than five thousand people were fed. They did not just have a taste of fish and bread, but each one ate until they were full – and there were even leftovers! What is going to happen in the area you are serving in this year? Will God multiply your efforts? I believe He will. I believe that He wants to do miracles. What will those miracles be? I do not know. That is His department. Our responsibility is to be available and to give all that we have to Jesus.

The final element of this lesson is that there were fragments left. Jesus told the disciples to gather up the fragments so that nothing was lost. I believe the fragments are those individuals who will hear our message but have not made a decision at that point. I believe that it will be critical to follow up with those individuals so that they are not "lost" to the kingdom. Those who have heard but have not committed themselves will need to be "gathered up" for more contact. We will need to get as much information as possible about them. We will also need to make sure that there will be "gatherers" to do the follow-up. This "gathering" of the fragments will also apply to those who have made decisions. If someone does not "gather" or follow up with them and get them tied into a Bible study, they are likely to drift back to their old ways.

Let each of us pray and give our all. Let each of us pray for God to do the miraculous because what we give will be touched by the Master. Let us each pray that these new babes in Christ, and those who are not yet disciples, will not be abandoned. O God, help us to be available until the task is complete.

Day 28

Important Questions

Isaiah 55

Incline your ear and come to Me. Listen, that you
may live; and I will make an everlasting covenant
with you, according to the faithful mercies shown
to David.
—Isaiah 55:3

In this passage we find some powerful questions asked of us
and some instructions directed to us that can help us as we
prepare ourselves to be used by God. We also find some great
promises that should encourage us to continue to prepare
ourselves to be vessels that God can use. We can witness to
others using the same questions that we ask ourselves, such as
"Why are you spending money on things that will not meet
your basic needs of love, peace, and forgiveness?" and "Why are
you spending so much energy on things that bring no eternal
satisfaction?"

Only Christ can satisfy our deepest longings and hunger.
As we listen to Him and come to Him (Isaiah 55:3), we will
hear and live. He will make an everlasting covenant with us.
I am so grateful that God loves us so much that He wants to
be involved in our lives. God wants to have mercy on us and
to forgive us of all our sins. Praise the Lord today for such a
wonderful, loving God who cares so much for us.

Another thing we find in this passage is that God is not
bound by our plans or even by our thoughts of what we think
He should do. We are His instruments, and as such, we do not

determine when or how we will be used. The Master determines when and how. God has a way of doing His thing, and it is always the right thing. In the course of serving God, we often experience God in ways that we did not expect. He brings divine appointment after divine appointment. He fulfills His plans in those we go to serve and on those who are being served. In the end, it is very common for the server to be the one served. In the end, we realize that His ways are higher than ours (Isaiah 55:9).

We are also to be ever mindful of the truths contained in verses 11-13 of our text. God's Word never returns to Him empty or void. It will accomplish what pleases God, and it will be successful in the matter that He sent it out to do (v. 11). Even God's creation rejoices in our efforts: *The mountains and the hills will break forth into shouts of joy before you, and all the trees of the field will clap their hands* (v. 12). As we are out doing God's work, He causes the hills and trees to rejoice. So when you are sharing the gospel and you hear the trees swaying, know that they are just praising the Lord because His people are busy getting God's Word out to a lost and dying world.

As you pray today, ask God to convince you that nothing we do for Him is ever wasted. We are preparing ourselves to be used by God to bring about singing and clapping, even of God's creation. Continue to pray and be drawn even closer to God so that He can use you in a mighty way.

The Enabling Christ

Philippians 4:10-23

My God will supply all your needs according to
His riches in glory in Christ Jesus.
—Philippians 4:19

The themes of Philippians are joy, entire consecration to Christ, and love for His church. Joy, however, seems to recur throughout. We can rejoice in the fact that through Christ we can have great joy and can be fully enabled by Him. This enablement will give each of us the assurances that will sustain us as we labor for Jesus Christ.

Paul said that because God is enabling him, he could be what he ought to be. He could also be content because of the presence of Christ in his life. Being content is not dependent on outward, favorable circumstances. The contentment Paul is talking about is like that described in Psalm 1 (please read). In this text, the psalmist said that contentment is like a tree planted by the rivers of water. This tree brings forth its fruit in the proper season, and its leaves do not wither. This tree is subject to the hot winds from the desert and the effects of those times of drought, just as the other trees that are away from the river. The difference is that this tree is able to defy those elements because it is continuously nourished by the life-giving waters that are flowing at its roots.

Each one of us, if Christ is living inside of us, has life-giving water continuously flowing to our "roots" because of our commitment to Jesus Christ by faith. Therefore, we can be what we ought to be because of Christ's presence in our lives. Christ can make us content and at peace because of His abiding in us.

Paul also said that because of the enabling Christ, we can do what we ought to do (Philippians 4:13). Christ gives us the strength to achieve what would otherwise be impossible. In Matthew 19:26, Jesus said that certain things are impossible with men, but that *with God all things are possible*. Christ also gives us the strength to endure what would otherwise be intolerable. Paul fully experienced this reality (see 2 Corinthians 11:24-28). We read of the physical and mental abuse that he endured. Without the indwelling and enabling Christ in Paul's life, he would have quit long before he finished, yet he kept on. Therefore, as he was about to be martyred, he could say, *I have fought the good fight, I have finished the course, I have kept the faith* (2 Timothy 4:7).

Finally, Paul said that through the enabling Christ, he could have what he ought to have. Paul knew that our God owns the cattle on a thousand hills (Psalm 50:10) and that He even owns the hills. God is able to supply every need that we have and will have. Paul did not say, "My God will supply all your wants," but he said, *My God will supply all your needs* (Philippians 4:19). I have experienced this over and over again during my life. God has provided financially for me just when it was needed. More than once, He has brought food to our table. One time God sent a man to our home with half of a beef cow. The man knocked on the door and asked if I would be offended if he gave me half of a beef. I replied, "No, not at all."

He smiled and announced, "Fine. Please help me unload it and we will put it in your freezer."

Because of the enabling Christ, we can each say, "Through Christ, I can." We each can claim what is ours in Christ. Spend some time today thanking God for giving us His Son, Jesus Christ, as well as the indwelling Holy Spirit.

Day 30

Here I Am. Send Me!

Isaiah 6:1-12

Then I heard the voice of the Lord, saying, "Whom shall I send, and who will go for Us?" Then I said, "Here am I. Send me!"
—Isaiah 6:8

Isaiah remembered the year well. It was marked in his memory as being the year that King Uzziah died, but he also remembered it for another reason. During that year he had a very deep worship experience with the real King, the Lord of Hosts. I pray that through this devotional, each of us has had a real worship experience with the Lord of Hosts. I pray that we have caught a vision of ourselves in all of our sinfulness, which is in stark contrast with the majesty and holiness of God. I hope that we have allowed the seraphim of God to purge us of our sins so that we have had a spiritual cleansing.

Isaiah heard the voice of God saying, *Whom shall I send, and who will go for Us?* Isaiah responded, *Here am I. Send me* (v. 8). Some people have read this passage and felt that the Lord had cornered and trapped Isaiah. What else could he say except to whimper, "Okay, Lord, I will do it."

I do not believe that is the correct understanding of this passage. I do not think that Isaiah felt trapped; rather, I believe he felt in awe of the whole situation. I believe that Isaiah was so grateful to see the Lord high and lifted up and to have his sins purged that his heart was bursting with joy. He was humbled before the Lord God Almighty, but then he was brought to a state that he had never experienced before. His sins had been forgiven and he was a new man.

When you experienced your new birth in Christ and your sins were forgiven, were you feeling trapped or was joy bursting forth from every pore of your body? I know the latter was true for me. When I received Christ's forgiveness, I wanted to shout it from the housetops. In fact, I could not be kept quiet. I told everyone I saw what had happened. This is how I think Isaiah felt. When he heard God ask, *Whom shall I send, and who will go for Us?* I think Isaiah was on his tiptoes shouting, *Here am I. Send me!*

I pray that as you have completed this devotional, you feel the same way and will be on your tiptoes saying, "Here, Lord – pick me! Please let me go. Send me, Lord, wherever You want to send me. Here I am. Please let me go!"

Part Three

Thirty-Day Reentry Devotional

Day 1

We Are Called to Be on Mission at Home

Matthew 28:18-20; Acts 1:8

Go therefore and make disciples of all the nations,
baptizing them in the name of the Father and the
Son and the Holy Spirit, teaching them to observe
all that I commanded you; and lo, I am with you
always, even to the end of the age.
—Matthew 28:19-20

It is easy to become farsighted when it comes to the concept of missions. We tend to think that missions is something that occurs overseas, in another country, or is the work of a church planter in the inner city of another state. We save, fundraise, plan, and strategize so we can spend a week detached from our everyday lives. We run away from our problems, our obligations, and our distractions and serve God from sunrise to sunset. Do not forget that coveted free day that is all about shopping, souvenirs, sightseeing, and eating out. The week is over, and our involvement in missions ceases – at least until next year.

Do not let this be the case for you as you return home, but let us remember the words of Jesus: *Go therefore and make disciples of all the nations.* The Greek word for "go" implies the act of making disciples, baptizing, and teaching "as you are going." It makes no distinction that we live in one location and then leave and go to another location to serve God, but we are to serve God as we go about our everyday routine. Acts 1:8 reminds us that we are empowered by the indwelling of the Holy Spirit. What are we empowered to do? We are empowered to be lights in the darkness, to proclaim the gospel in a *crooked and perverse generation* (Philippians 2:15). We are called to be witnesses not only in the far-off country, but also right here in our own Jerusalem.

From the Greek word *matereo*, we get our English word "martyr," which is translated as "witness" in this passage. The same Spirit who has sustained you and strengthened you as you served this past week is the same Spirit who will give you the courage to stand with the courage of a martyr when you return home. Historically, a martyr is someone who will uphold what is right and holy when everyone else is content to bow down to the false idols of our world. They stand before the statue unwilling to bend the knee and willing to face the fire so that God's name may be exalted.

We are commanded and empowered to be witnesses not only in Samaria and to the remotest part of the earth, but also right at home in the heart of Jerusalem. Will you be willing to stand up and proclaim the gospel when you are standing before your cynical coworker instead of the child at the orphanage? Will you share the truth of God's Word with the reluctant parent on your son's travel team as opposed to the single mom living in the one-room hut in the Honduran village? Every Christian is called to be a missionary every day.

Dance Before the Lord

2 Samuel 6:12-23

So David said to Michal, "It was before the LORD, who chose me above your father and above all his house, to appoint me ruler over the people of the LORD, over Israel; therefore I will celebrate before the LORD."
—2 Samuel 6:21

You will learn very quickly that many people here in the United States do not have the same hunger and passion for God and His Word as those whom you just left. It was so refreshing to be among people who could not get enough of God's Word and who were not constantly on their phones or watching the clock. Every time I return home from a mission trip, whether it was in the inner city of Memphis, on Native American reservations, or in another country, it always takes me a few weeks to process the apathy of the church in regard to spiritual depth and lostness. I make it a goal to go on a mission trip once a year just to keep the fire burning brightly in my own life and to be reminded that God has blessed me in ways I cannot even imagine.

I feel very much like David in 2 Samuel 6:12 when he saw the blessings that God's presence was having on the house of Obed-edom and desired that same blessing for himself and Israel. He was so overjoyed as the ark of the covenant entered Jerusalem that David danced in the streets to glorify Yahweh (2 Samuel 6:20-21). It is normal to come home excited and ready to serve God. It is perfectly understandable that you would want to keep the fire burning and tell as many people as you can about the awesome God you serve. The sad reality is that your enthusiasm will not likely receive the welcome that you hope. This world is full of the "Michals" of Samuel's day who are quick to criticize, tear down, and try to cause others to question the joy and boldness that they are experiencing.

Some of the emotions that I have experienced after a mission trip included disappointment, depression, frustration, confusion, and most frequently, anger and fear. I was angry that no one cared, that no one desired to grow, that everyone was too busy, and that God was not a priority to them, but only a convenience. After my anger subsided, I was afraid that I would fall back into the complacency and apathy around me.

Let your attitude be the same as David's when he said, *I will be more lightly esteemed than this and will be humble in my own eyes* (2 Samuel 6:22). David was telling us that he did not care what he looked like or what others thought of him. If worshiping and glorifying God made him look foolish, then a fool he would be. Do not get discouraged when the excitement you bring home falls on deaf ears and cold hearts, but continue to dance before the Lord.

Day 3

Weeping over the Lost

Luke 19:41-44

When He approached Jerusalem, He saw the city
and wept over it.
—Luke 19:41

If we could see the future of the majority of the people with
whom we come in contact, then we would weep in the same
way as Jesus. He lifted His eyes toward Jerusalem and saw the
judgment that was coming upon it. He saw the destruction of
the temple, of the city, and of parents and their children. In
His sovereignty and omniscience, He knew that many people
would reject His coming, His sacrifice, and His offer of salvation – and it brought our Savior to tears.

There is no doubt in my mind that you have become more
aware of the lostness and helplessness of those in your hometown. It is a reality that may have eluded us before because we
had become comfortable with and ignorant to the sinfulness
around us. The behavior of our coworkers, the impassiveness of
our family, and the laziness of our church had all become com-
monplace. However, your experience on your mission trip and
your encounter with God and what He can do with a willing
servant has removed the rose-colored glasses from your eyes.

You may be feeling alone and think that you are unable to
do anything about the spiritual condition you see all around
you. It is okay to feel this way. It is okay to weep and grieve for
those around you who are heading toward an eternity separated
from God's love and holiness.

Ask God for comfort and strength. Call out the lost by name and ask God to use you to draw them unto Himself.

My son came home one day from school after trying to share the gospel with one of his friends. He told me that his friend said he believed in God. After a few minutes, I discovered that this friend did not believe in the God of Scripture, and he had been deceived. As I was communicating the fact to my eleven-year-old son that his friend was an unbeliever in need of Christ, I saw the look on his face. I would imagine it was a similar look that Jesus had when He approached Jerusalem and saw its future. Later that evening as I walked by my son's room, I heard the emotion in his voice as he prayed for his friend to come to know Jesus as his Lord and Savior.

Be grateful that your eyes have been opened, and do not let this world close them again. Yes, it is more painful and is a heavy burden to see and feel the lostness around you. However, it will also remind you daily that the mission of proclaiming the gospel is not over, but has just begun.

A City Full of Idols

Acts 17:16-22

Now while Paul was waiting for them at Athens,
his spirit was being provoked within him as he was
observing the city full of idols.
—Acts 17:16

I know that many times after you return from vacation, a mission trip, or a weekend getaway, you need time to relax before you head back to the everyday grind. It is our tendency to settle back into our routine and leave the missions until our next event or trip. Paul had a similar situation in Acts 17, when he was waiting in Athens with nothing to do. His friends were finishing up ministry in Berea, and for safety reasons Paul traveled ahead to the next city.

As Paul looked around, all he could see was a city full of idolatry, and his spirit was provoked. He became restless and tortured by the thought of the grip that sin had on this city and its people. It was impossible for him to sit by and simply wait when he knew that he had the cure for their disease. He knew that Jesus was the cure. He visited the synagogue, and then made his way to the marketplace. Word began to spread about the message that Paul was preaching. He was invited into the academic world of Mars Hill, and there Paul started at the beginning and used their own culture to boldly proclaim the good news of Jesus.

It is okay for you to take a day to catch your breath and absorb everything that God did through you and within you while you were on your mission trip. Just remember that the job is not done, but the mission has only begun. Listen for the moments when God provokes your spirit, and respond with obedience. The reason why Paul went to the synagogue and the marketplace was because there were people there – people who needed to hear the gospel. There are people at your work, at your school, at the ball games, and at the campgrounds who need to be introduced to Jesus Christ. Take a hot shower, spend some time in prayer, and get a good night's rest – because tomorrow you have work to do.

Do Not Diminish God's Ability to Use You

Exodus 3-4

"Therefore, come now, and I will send you to
Pharoah, so that you may bring My people, the
sons of Israel, out of Egypt." But Moses said to
God, "Who am I, that I should go to Pharaoh, and
that I should bring the sons of Israel out of Egypt?"
And He said, "Certainly I will be with you, and
this shall be the sign to you that it is I who have
sent you; when you have brought the people out of
Egypt, you shall worship God at this mountain."
—Exodus 3:10-12

There are a lot of things that irritate me, but none more than
people who constantly make excuses. I constantly hear
from friends who either run a business or manage a department about the numerous times employees fail to show up to
work and deliver an excuse for the fifth time that month. I
work with a lot of volunteers, and I become frustrated when
someone commits to a job and then cancels at the last minute
with some excuse.

In Exodus 3, God called out to Moses from the burning
bush. God explained to Moses the situation in Egypt, which
Moses was aware of, and told him that He planned to use him
to deliver His people from their affliction. This should have
been exciting news. Wasn't this exactly what Moses was trying
to do forty years earlier when he rescued the Israelite from the
Egyptian (Exodus 2:11-13)? God even promised to accompany

Moses on his journey and in his efforts. However, Moses began to pour out the excuses, making a list of all the reasons why he was incapable of accomplishing what God was asking of him:

- Who am I that I should go to Pharaoh?

- Who will I say has sent me?

- What if they do not believe me?

- I have never been a man of words. *I am slow of speech and slow of tongue* (Exodus 4:10).

God has an answer for every excuse.

- *I will be with you* (Exodus 3:12).

- I AM – Yahweh – *the God of your fathers, the God of Abraham, the God of Isaac, and the God of Jacob has sent me to you* (Exodus 3:15).

- God caused Moses to use his staff to perform miracles so that they would believe that Yahweh had appeared to him (Exodus 4:2-5).

- *Who has made man's mouth? . . . Is it not I, the LORD? Now then go, and I, even I, will be with your mouth, and teach you what you are to say* (Exodus 4:11-12).

Moses could only see his flaws and weaknesses. He knew the words he wanted to say, but they would not flow from his mouth. His low self-esteem kept him from seeing his potential as a leader. He did not believe anyone would follow him if he did lead.

You may be feeling the same way. It has almost been a week, and you have seen more discouragement than encouragement. The team you were so close with last week is nowhere to be seen, and you have barely heard from them. You are questioning whether you are capable of being the Christian at home that you were last week.

We have the benefit of knowing the results that Moses did

not know at the burning bush. We know that God raised up Aaron to walk beside him and that Moses became a powerful and effective leader. Despite all his weaknesses, perceived flaws, and excuses, God used Moses for forty years and fulfilled every promise He made. Do not diminish God's ability to use you.

Day 6

No Honor at Home

Mark 6:4

Jesus said to them, "A prophet is not without honor except in his hometown and among his own relatives and in his own household."
—Mark 6:4

Wasn't it a wonderful feeling to be welcomed, accepted, listened to, and appreciated? I remember my first foreign mission trip to Brazil. There was a little girl who followed me everywhere I went and just hung on my arm. I was seventeen and she was probably six or seven, and she loved teaching me new Portuguese words. She would run through the village and let everyone know that they needed to come and listen to her new friends.

I am guessing you have similar stories you could share about the children who clung to your leg, hung on your arm, or climbed up into your lap. You could talk about the small church filled with people eager to hear God's Word, hanging on every verse you read and every story you told. You could recall the mother and two small children who walked several miles just to hear you share your testimony or to listen to the pastor's sermon. It is refreshing to know that God is at work and that He used you to make an eternal impact on someone's life.

It has been six days since you have been home. Have you felt it yet? Are you starting to see that even though God is still at work, the miracles seem to be less frequent? Are you beginning to realize that no one is following you around hungry for God's Word and willing to listen? There are no rooms filled to capacity and no families traveling miles to be spiritually fed. You are finding it difficult to convince people to choose Christ over the many other things on their agenda.

You might feel as if you are the only one going through this, but you are not. Your team members are probably struggling with these same emotions, and so did Jesus. Everywhere Jesus went, He attracted a crowd. He taught five thousand men, in addition to women and children. He spoke in a house so full that the only way in was to open a hole in the roof. He taught on a beach so crowded that He had to stand in a boat to address the multitude. However, when He went back home to Nazareth, He marveled at their unbelief, and His ministry was hindered due to their lack of faith (Mark 6:5-6).

Jesus did not let this one experience slow Him down. Instead, He healed those who came to Him and He set His eyes toward the next village. He gathered His disciples and sent them out ahead of Him to prepare the hearts of the people for harvest. So if you are not experiencing the same appreciation or zeal as you did last week, that is okay. Set your eyes on the next task, make a plan for tomorrow, and be obedient today.

True Power Comes Only from God

Acts 8:4-13

> But when they believed Philip preaching the good
> news about the kingdom of God and the name of
> Jesus Christ, they were being baptized, men and
> women alike.
> —Acts 8:12

It might seem as if the task before you is too much for you to handle by yourself, and the answer is, "You're right." We are designed by God to be relational creatures. We thrive when we are with other believers in a local church. We need to develop a small circle of friends who will challenge us, hold us accountable, and be ready to help if we need them. To paraphrase Ecclesiastes 4:9-12, two are better than one, and three are better than two. We are stronger together.

While unity is extremely important, more than that is required to provide the strength and power we need to accomplish what God has placed before us. Some of the first people to walk on earth thought they could achieve greatness by joining together and building a tower to heaven so that their name would be made great (Genesis 11). We know what happened to them. God confused their language and scattered them throughout the earth. True power does not come from within us. It cannot be produced by human achievements or by the joint efforts of like-minded people. True power comes from God.

Philip found himself in Samaria, a place that had never heard this beautiful message of Jesus Christ. For years the people there had been astonished and amazed by a sorcerer named Simon. God's Word tells us that Simon claimed to be someone great (Acts 8:9) and that the people called him *the Great Power of God* (v. 10). However, when Philip showed up and started preaching Christ to them, the people begin to realize that Philip possessed true power. The people began to see the falseness of Simon and the truth of Jesus Christ. Simon even realized that God was providing something that he had never been able to provide himself.

If you have repented and trusted in Christ as your Lord and Savior, then you are filled with and sealed by the Holy Spirit of God. Your body has become the temple of the living God, and you possess the same power as Philip. All throughout the book of Acts, you will read the phrase *filled with the Spirit*. The Greek understanding of this phrase is not that one is receiving an additional dose of the Spirit, but that we are surrendering our wills to that of God's will and allowing the Spirit to work within us uninhibitedly. You are fully capable of handling the task God has placed before you. You are perfectly equipped to stand up against the apathy, grief, idols, doubt, and lack of appreciation – because it is not you! Only Christ in you can empower this kind of boldness.

Day 8

Do Not Let Unbelief Rob You of the Promised Land

Numbers 13-14

Then Caleb quieted the people before Moses, and said, "We should by all means go up and take possession of it, for we shall surely overcome it." But the men who had gone up with him said, "We are not able to go up against the people, for they are too strong for us." So they gave out to the sons of Israel a bad report of the land which they had spied out. —Numbers 13:30-32

M any pastors would share a saying with me when they told me stories of a difficult church or ministry where they had previously served. They would say, "God called me to be a Moses to prepare that church for their Joshua." I understood what they meant, and at times I have felt that way about places where I have served, but there is a major flaw in this logic. Moses was not allowed to enter the promised land because of an act of disobedience. The same thing happened to the ten spies who doubted, and to the people of Israel who listened to them. None of these people were allowed to enter the promised land.

I do not know about you, but if I am going to put my blood, sweat, and tears into the mission of proclaiming Christ in my home, work, church, and community, then I would like to be there to enjoy the fruits of my labor and to experience the blessings God has promised to those who remain faithful. I do not want my unbelief and disobedience to force me to pass the blessing on to someone else.

There have been more times than I would like to admit in which someone returned from a mission trip on fire for the Lord, only to have the embers die after a few weeks. They may have led someone to the Lord, received Christ themselves, or simply allowed God to grow them by means of their daily obedience. Then the return home was filled with voices of unbelief. Your spouse is cynical, your church is apathetic, your coworkers are not interested, your friends are too busy, your boss calls it a vacation, and your Facebook posts only gather a handful of "likes" – and you decide to listen to the voices.

You feel the weight of the world, the hopelessness, the lost-ness, the darkness of millions of people who have never heard the gospel and are perishing every single day. You come back home to a family, a community, and a church family that does not seem to care. This is how Joshua and Caleb felt when they returned to the people of Israel. They remained faithful, but had to endure forty years of wandering in the wilderness because of the unbelief of the other spies who swayed the people.

You need to have a louder voice than the doubters. You need to rally the troops back to God's Word. It is up to you to remind the other followers of Christ of His promises. You need to remind them of the blessings rather than the obstacles.

Start with Prayer

Nehemiah 1:4-2:4

When I heard these words, I sat down and wept
and mourned for days; and I was fasting and praying before the God of heaven.
—Nehemiah 1:4

It must have been strange for Nehemiah to hear the devastating news of the situation in Jerusalem. There had been seventy
years of stories about the majesty of the temple, the beauty of its
gates, and the fortified walls. It was once the center of religion
and commerce, but decades later there had been no efforts to
rebuild it, and the people of God were struggling.

I can imagine that when you return home and see the state
of your country, community, and church you may be ready to
tear your clothes and fall on your knees before God. This would
be the right response! There is nothing you will be able to do in
your own strength that will change the hearts of those around
you. You need help. You need God.

The first thing Nehemiah did when he heard the news of
Jerusalem was to pray. He confessed his sin and the sin of all of
Israel. He poured out his heart before God. This prayer is not
limited to one single prayer that occurred only in a moment of
great emotional stress, but rather it was a continued brokenness
that lasted for a number of days. We see in Nehemiah 2 that
rebuilding Jerusalem was a burden that was still on Nehemiah's
heart and mind three months later. It was hard for him to be
joyful when his kinsmen were hurting. It was difficult for him

to be content in the palace when he knew that God's people were exposed and vulnerable to their enemies. His face could not hide the pain in his heart. Others asked Nehemiah what was wrong, and what did he do? He prayed.

You may be disappointed, frustrated, upset, afraid, heart-broken, insecure, or struggling in some other way with the broken-down walls and the gates that lie in ruins. The first thing you need to do is to pray. Pray for the believers to feel the urgency that you feel. Pray for the church to have a burden to reach the lost in their community. Pray for the courage to lead the way and step up when God opens the door. Follow Nehemiah's example: start with prayer.

Day 10

Praying for One Another

Colossians 1:9-14

For this reason also, since the day we heard of it, we
have not ceased to pray for you and to ask that you
may be filled with the knowledge of His will in all
spiritual wisdom and understanding, so that you
will walk in a manner worthy of the Lord, to please
Him in all respects, bearing fruit in every good
work and increasing in the knowledge of God.
—Colossians 1:9-10

You likely returned home from your mission trip with at least
one or two people with whom you shared experiences, and
you can be there for each other post-mission. If this is not the
case, then I encourage you to find one or two people who will
commit to be your prayer partner. It will be essential that you
are praying for other believers and that they are praying for you.

Paul tells us that we are to be praying for our brothers and
sisters in Christ to be filled with the knowledge of His will,
to walk in such a way that is pleasing to God, to bear fruit, to
endure, and to be patient, joyful, and full of thanksgiving. This
is my prayer for you right now as you are reading this devotional. I know the struggles that people face as they return home
because I have experienced them myself. I wish I would have
had someone to pray with and for me. It was a struggle for me
to keep the desire to continue growing in the knowledge of His
will after the week was over and my team, my support group,
was gone. It was a challenge for me to remain joyful and full

of thanksgiving when every effort I made to spread the gospel was met with unenthusiastic and reluctant responses.

Calling out the names of your brothers and sisters before God is crucial. There are also appropriate times to send a text or make a call to let those friends know that you have been praying for them. You do not need to make a big scene and stand on the street corner and shout your prayers for all to hear. Jesus warns us of the dangers of such prayers. However, to let your fellow believers know that they are not alone will encourage and strengthen you both.

Who can you start praying for today? Is it someone who went on your mission trip with you? Do you have someone praying for you? Who are you going to ask? It does not matter when you start, only that you do. Why not start today?

Day 11

Resolve in Your Heart

Daniel 1:8

But Daniel made up his mind [proposed in his heart] that he would not defile himself.
—Daniel 1:8

It is a guarantee that we will face difficulties in our efforts to live a godly life. Peter tells us, *Do not be surprised at the fiery ordeal among you* (1 Peter 4:12). Paul warned Timothy, *All who desire to live godly in Christ Jesus will be persecuted*

(2 Timothy 3:12). James reminds us that it is not *if* we face trials that we should be joyful, but *when* (James 1:2).

There was no greater trial for Daniel and his friends than to be ripped apart from their families and homes and hauled off to a foreign land. The Babylonians changed their names and hijacked their education. When they tried to force Daniel and his friends to sin against God by breaking the Levitical dietary laws, Daniel stood his ground. Some may wonder why Daniel drew the line at dietary rules. However, if you consider Jewish law, their name and choice in literature were insignificant; there were no restrictions in God's Word forbidding such things. In contrast, the king's dietary rules were a blatant violation of God's law, which Daniel would not break.

It is worth noticing that Daniel did not come to the resolution in the spur of the moment. This was a conviction of the heart that was grounded in his faith. Before the fall of Jerusalem and the journey as captives to Babylon, Daniel had decided that there were clear boundaries of obedience and disobedience. Andy Stanley wrote a Bible study that states that we should all have guardrails (boundaries) in our lives. Guardrails give us clarity about the location of the edge of the road and the dangers that lay beyond. The rumble strip that causes your car to shake is designed to alert the driver to be cautious.

Before we face exile, we need to determine in our hearts and minds where we stand. It is too late to respond when the car is crashing through the guardrail and tumbling into the ditch. We are to stand upon God's Word and pray, as both of these things keep us connected to God. We align ourselves so that He can clearly communicate through His Word and Spirit.

It would be easy for you to allow the apathy and hopelessness of the circumstances at home to extinguish the flame of revival that was ignited in your heart. It is at this moment that you must make a choice. Will you stand on God's Word and resolve in your heart and mind that you will not move no matter what may come? Will you put up guardrails and rumble strips, accountability partners, and other safeguards that will warn you when you stray from God's path? Will you willingly be the guardrail or rumble strip for a brother or sister who is trying to follow God's Word?

Day 12

Always Have a Plan

Nehemiah 2:7-17

Then the king said to me, "What would you request?" So I prayed to the God of heaven. I said to the king, "If it please the king, and if your servant has found favor before you, send me to Judah, to the city of my fathers' tombs, that I may rebuild it." —Nehemiah 2:4-5

Now that you know where you stand and have saturated your life in prayer, you are ready to look forward. Did you catch that? I said, "Look forward." Nehemiah had heard that Jerusalem was still in *great distress* (Nehemiah 1:3), and he was moved to prayer. He prayed for three months before God opened a door of opportunity for him to move out of his current situation.

This is probably one of the most challenging things I have faced in my life – waiting. Abraham waited twenty-five years. The Israelites waited four hundred years in Egypt, and then they waited another forty years in the wilderness. God does things in His own way and in His own time. We need to remain faithfully active instead of waiting passively for something to change.

Nehemiah was creating a game plan. He knew what needed to be done and what resources he needed to do it. Jerusalem needed a wall so the people there could be safe and secure from their enemies. Nehemiah asked for a letter so he could obtain the required lumber, and another letter seeking a security escort through enemy territory. God provided for both of his needs.

The first thing he did when he arrived in Jerusalem was to examine the condition of the wall and gates so he could put together a plan. If you need proof that Nehemiah was organized, then just read chapter 3, and you will see that he designated every tribe and available Israelite to a gate or portion of the wall for repair. Even when they were threatened by the enemy, the work did not stop – because Nehemiah had a plan for that situation as well.

Do not get in a hurry to run into the next phase of your life. Enjoy where God has placed you in this moment because He has you there for a reason. Look forward and begin making preparations for what you believe God is doing next, but do not get lost in tomorrow and forget to be faithful today. I know that waiting is hard, especially when you are ready to move, but be patient. God will open the door of opportunity when the time is right.

Doing What's Right When Nobody Else Is

Daniel 3

If it be so, our God whom we serve is able to
deliver us form the furnace of blazing fire; and He
will deliver us out of your hand, O king. But even
if He does not, let it be known to you, O king, that
we are not going to serve your gods or worship the
golden image that you have set up.
—Daniel 3:17-18

What does the door of opportunity look like? I bet it is new
and shiny with all the bells and whistles. Could it be a
new job with a bigger paycheck or a fresh start in a new town? It
is possible that it could be an opportunity to serve overseas on
missions or to serve weekly at your church. We generally think
of it as something better than our current situation; however,
this is not what God promises us.

Daniel had been promoted, and his friends had been left
behind to face an impossible challenge from the king. Shadrach,
Meshach, and Abed-nego were commanded to bow down to
a golden statue that stood ninety to a hundred feet high and
give their allegiance to Nebuchadnezzar. This is one of those
moments in which you needed to have made this decision in
your heart and mind before standing before all of Babylon. This
was not the first time that these three young men had taken
a stand for what was right, but this was the first time it was
so public. It was one thing to stand in the corner of the room

and talk to the captain of the guard in private, and something else entirely to stare down the king, his officials, and soldiers.

If all of this was not enough for us to understand what was going on, then imagine standing in the middle of a football stadium that was filled with people on the field and in the stands, with everyone bowing down except you. Most people would have you believe that because you are in the minority, you must be wrong. It will take courage to stand when everyone else is bowing, and to bow before God when everyone else is standing. I love the statement that Shadrach, Meshach, and Abed-nego made in verse 18: *But even if He does not [deliver us], let it be known to you, O king, that we are not going to serve your gods or worship the golden image.*

Even if. Will you stand and do the right thing even if the outcome is not what you desire? Will you proclaim Christ as Lord even if no one will listen? When your friends discourage you and your coworkers mock you, will you continue to be faithful to God? When the whole world is watching, or maybe even just your family, will you do what is right?

Day 14

Doing What's Right When Nobody's Looking

Daniel 6:10-24

Now when Daniel knew that the document was
signed, he entered his house (now in his roof
chamber he had windows open toward Jerusalem);
and he continued kneeling on his knees three
times a day, praying and giving thanks before his
God, as he had been doing previously.
—Daniel 6:10

You have gotten back from your trip and the team has all
gone their separate ways. Sunday morning has come and
gone. The songs have been sung and the sermon is over. You
have clocked out of work for the weekend. Your wife is away
with the kids visiting family and there is no one around but
you. This is a whole different type of temptation and pressure
that is not coming from other people, but from within. There
is an opportunity to sin, and the only ones who would know
about it would be you and God.

There are a lot of believers who will put on a strong front
and pretend like they have it all together. They are the model
Christians, ideal parents, faithful servants, and knowledgeable
teachers – and secretly a total mess. We are called to be people
of integrity who remain faithful to God no matter if everyone
is watching or no one is. Daniel was a man of integrity.

The satraps, governors of the provinces, convinced King

Darius to issue a decree that all of Babylon must pray to him alone for thirty days. This was done because the satraps knew that Daniel prayed faithfully to his God three times each day. Daniel's prayer life was not something he did in a boastful manner or in a public place, but in the privacy of his own home. He could have easily adhered to the king's decree for thirty days, and no one would have been the wiser. He knew the document had been signed, yet he still prayed and gave thanks before his God, as he had done previously. Daniel did not change a thing. It did not matter who else knew, because he would know – and so would God.

Nobody is watching, so you could easily click on that website, have an affair, take a little money from the register, go to lunch without clocking out, have a little too much to drink, or send that inappropriate message to your old classmate. No one will know.

Wrong! God knows. If you ever plan to truly make an impact on this lost and dying world, then you must be faithful to God when no one is looking. You must live for God past Sunday morning and beyond the one week of missions each year. You must proclaim Christ from the rooftops and praise Him behind closed doors.

Day 15

Trials Produce Steadfastness

James 1:1-8

Consider it all joy, my brethren, when you encounter various trials, knowing that the testing of your faith produces endurance.
—James 1:2-3

James is writing this letter predominately to Christians with a Jewish heritage. These believers are well acquainted with hardships and persecution since they have been scattered from their home because of their faith in Jesus. I am sure it was a surprise to his readers when they came to verse 2 and saw the word *joy*. The phrase *the testing of your faith* took them back to when Abraham was asked to offer Isaac as an offering to God. It had to be a challenge for Abraham to suppress the emotions he was feeling as he took the three-day journey to the mountain where he would lay a knife to the flesh of his only son. I imagine you are feeling a lot of emotions right now after trying to make sense of the past few weeks. Let me say that you are not alone and that what you are experiencing is very normal. It is concerning when people come home from a week or two of intense mission work and return to life as usual as if they had not witnessed God do a great work.

There is good news. James reminds us that the struggles we are facing will produce something wonderful: steadfastness. He is telling us that on the other side of your trial is a more mature version of yourself that is a clearer reflection of Christ. We take one more step toward perfection. There is more good news. If we are having trouble navigating our trial, then all we have to do is ask God for wisdom and He will give it to us. There is one caveat: we must ask in faith without doubt. We must believe that God is who He says He is and will do what He says He will do.

This is where you will have to become a little nostalgic and travel back in time a few weeks. Try to recall those times when God showed up and performed a miracle, such as the storm that dropped rain everywhere except where you were serving, or the small amount of food that somehow never ended. Remember the smiles on the children's faces as they heard the gospel and responded with repentance of sins and trust in Jesus as Lord. The same God who did all those things will give you wisdom. The same God who transformed those children's lives will carry you through your trial and produce within you a faithful and steadfast heart.

Live Holy as Strangers in This World – His Word, His People

1 Peter 1:13-2:12

But like the Holy One who called you, be holy
yourselves also in all your behavior; because it is
written, "You shall be holy, for I am holy."
—1 Peter 1:15-16

There are several things that believers need in their lives, but two of the most important are God's Word and a biblical community. Peter is writing this letter to the persecuted believers who have been scattered throughout the region. The first response when you are faced with difficulties and trials is to withdraw and live in isolation. It would have been easy for the first-century Christians to practice their faith in the privacy of their homes and live incognito among the public. There was just one problem: God had called them, and has called us, to be witnesses to the lost nations.

God *has called [us] out of the darkness into His marvelous light* (1 Peter 2:9). We are to abstain from the lusts of this world and live in such a way that our good deeds can be seen, and so God is glorified through our lives (2:11-12). God's Word commands us to be people of action (1:13), obedience (1:14), and holiness (1:15-16). All these verses remind us that we are not to live in the shadows; rather, we are to stand in His light, and we are to be the light. This is challenging to do, but remember that we have been made new creations in Christ and have been born not only of flesh, but also of the Spirit. We no longer belong in the world, but are strangers in a foreign land. Philippians 3:20 tells us, *Our citizenship is in heaven, from which also we eagerly wait for a Savior, the Lord Jesus Christ.*

How are we to survive the struggles of the world? What has God given us to enable us to live holy lives? We were born again *through the living and enduring word of God* (1 Peter 1:23). The Word of God is what is needed to renew our minds daily in order to keep us from conforming to this world. It is impossible to grow closer to Christ without being in His Word. God tells us that those who love Him will obey His commandments (John 14:15). The reality is that you cannot obey commandments that you do not know, and therefore you are unable to love God as He has commanded. If we want to love God and live holy lives, we must be growing in His Word. You can take the temperature of your relationship with Christ by determining whether you are still drinking the milk of God's Word or eating spiritual steak.

The second thing that God has given us to help us live a life of obedience is family. I am not necessarily talking about your blood relatives, but your spiritual family, the church. It is imperative that you are involved with other believers. Peter reminded the scattered persecuted Christians that they were not alone. They were *living stones, . . . built up as a spiritual house for a holy priesthood, to offer up spiritual sacrifices acceptable to God through Jesus Christ* (1 Peter 2:5). They are *a chosen race, a royal priesthood, a holy nation, a people for God's own possession* (1 Peter 2:9). God created us to be relational creatures, and we are called to live out our faith as a community of believers. We are to encourage one another, rebuke one another, confess our sins, bear each other's burden, pick each other up when we stumble, and pray for one another.

Are you spending time reading the Bible every day? Is the

Bible your standard to which you measure everything else? Are you satisfied drinking milk, or are you diving deeper into His Word, ready for God to reveal His amazing mystery to you? Are you connected to a local body of believers? Are you plugged into a small group or Bible study with other followers of Christ? Are you engaged and serving alongside the body of Christ? What changes do you need to make?

Day 17

God Makes Living a Holy Life Possible

Philippians 2:12-17

For it is God who is at work in you, both to will
and to work for His good pleasure.
—Philippians 2:13

There is no denying that we live in *a crooked and perverse generation* (Philippians 2:15). It is a reality that becomes more evident after each election and politically charged riot. We see our schools teaching false doctrine and permitting immoral behavior. Our churches have become more like dog and pony shows than houses of prayer. Pastors have become storytellers and motivational speakers whose agenda is to fill pews, not to transform people from death to life. The first thing that must happen is a reality check – a wake-up call to our present condition.

The second thing that must take place is an acknowledgement

that in the midst of the darkness of this world, we are the light (v. 15). We are to be blameless and innocent. Before you say that this is an impossible task, let me just say that I agree. If we are attempting to be holy and above reproach in our own strength, then yes, our efforts are in vain. However, there is hope! God reminds us that while we are the ones who are working out our salvation, it is God who saved us by His righteous act on the cross. It is God who promises us that He is working through us to accomplish His will and His work (v. 13). Matthew 19:26 says, *With people this is impossible, but with God all things are possible.*

God never promised us that living a holy life would be easy, but He does tell us that if we hold fast to the Word of God and pour out our lives as drink offerings to God, then we can rejoice with Christ, for our lives were not lived in vain (Philippians 2:16-17).

So what does this mean for me? It means that what I do and why I do it matters. It means that I need to build my life on the right foundation: Jesus. Everything that is built upon that foundation needs to be done *for His good pleasure* (v. 13). Will what I build upon the foundation of my life stand on the day of judgment as I stand before Christ (1 Corinthians 3:10-15)? Will my works be a product of my own efforts and desires, or will they be the product of the Holy Spirit working within me? I must constantly answer this question in my own life, as you should do in yours.

All Is Lost Without Christ

Philippians 3:1-14

But whatever things were gain to me, those things I have counted as loss for the sake of Christ. More than that, I count all things to be loss in view of the surpassing value of knowing Christ Jesus my Lord, for whom I have suffered the loss of all things, and count them but rubbish so that I may gain Christ.
—Philippians 3:7-8

D id you answer the questions from yesterday? Will my works be a product of my own efforts and desires, or will they be the product of the Holy Spirit working within me? Are you having a hard time deciphering whether your works are man-made or divinely inspired?

Paul gives us a glimpse into the transformation from his old life to his new, abundant life. He starts off by listing all his accomplishments, and it is a very impressive list. In society's eyes, Paul had the right heritage, the right pedigree, the best education, a spotless record, and was on the fast track to the top of his field. According to the world, life did not get any better than the one Paul was living as he traveled to Damascus.

However, in verse 7 we get to see what Paul Harvey would call "the rest of the story." The apostle Paul was transformed by Christ. He was blinded and then given new sight. He was confused, but later all things were made clear. He was dead in his sins, yet he became alive in Christ. After his encounter with Christ, he realized that everything that the world celebrated was truly as significant as manure. Jesus asked, *What does it profit a man to gain the whole world, and forfeit his soul?* (Mark 8:36). Paul learned that to have everything the world has to offer without having Christ resulted in an empty and purposeless life. If we are not careful, we will fall into the snare of this world and find value in the wrong places and things.

There is another truth that we must remember as we attempt to live holy lives. We are not perfect, and we will never attain perfection on this side of heaven. That does not mean that we are not to strive to live lives that are pleasing to God. It will be a daily challenge to turn away from the things of this world and seek after righteousness, but rejecting sin and pursuing righteousness is worth it. The moment you trusted Christ as your Lord and Savior, you became an adopted child of God, an heir to eternal life, and your citizenship was transferred to heaven. There is no earthly possession or achievement that will satisfy the longing in your heart that is looking toward your heavenly home.

This World Is Sinful, but This Is Not Our Home

Philippians 3:17-21

For our citizenship is in heaven, from which also we eagerly wait for a Savior, the Lord Jesus Christ; who will transform the body of our humble state into conformity with the body of His glory, by the exertion of the power that He has even to subject all things to Himself.
—Philippians 3:20-21

This is not your home. You do not belong here. It is a temporary rental property while your eternal home is being prepared. Jesus told His disciples that He was leaving so that He could go and prepare a place for them. One day He will come back to receive His bride, the church, and take us to the new heaven and new earth. Jesus left His followers behind and entrusted them with the gospel to make disciples, baptize, and teach others all that He had commanded them. We have a mission to accomplish, and that mission will never be fulfilled as long as we are consumed with an earthly appetite. We must set our minds and our hearts on heavenly things (Philippians 3:19).

If you have ever taken a vacation, then you know how wonderful it is to forget about home for a little while. You do not have to worry about cleaning, cooking, running errands, transporting your kids to their activities, or the never-ending demands of the routine that tomorrow may hold for you. Instead, you simply enjoy the beach, restaurants, theme parks, and your days filled with absolutely nothing but rest.

If you are anything like me, however, you begin to miss home about five or six days into vacation. There are things that are just too wonderful to forget, such as your bed, or your dog curling up beside you. You begin to miss movie night with the family, and your refrigerator that is full of snacks. Yes, being home comes with responsibilities, but the benefits are far greater.

In a similar way, we are living life on vacation; but for believers, there should be an intense longing to go home. We are to desire that sabbath rest that belongs only to those who have trusted Christ. We should be tired of the brokenness of this world and should be ready to be transformed *into conformity with the body of His glory* (vv. 20-21). As we eagerly wait for Christ to return, we are to actively strive to accomplish our kingdom mission. We can do this by reminding ourselves that every person we encounter is someone in need of the gospel. There are people all around us who are separated from God and need to be reconciled back to Him. God has made us new creations so that we can become His ambassadors of reconciliation (2 Corinthians 5:17-20). This may not be our home, but while we are here, we have work to do.

Contentment in Christ

Philippians 4:10-15

Not that I speak from want, for I have learned to
be content in whatever circumstances I am. I know
how to get along with humble means, and I also
know how to live in prosperity; in any and every
circumstance I have learned the secret of being
filled and going hungry, both of having abundance
and suffering need. I can do all things through
Him who strengthens me.
—Philippians 4:11-13

Jeremiah the prophet tells us that trying to find satisfaction
in this world is meaningless. He describes it as pouring water
into a cistern that is broken. Trying to find satisfaction apart
from Christ is like trying to pull water up from a well with
a bucket filled with holes. It is a pointless task, but for some
reason we keep trying to find contentment in all the wrong
places. Paul provides a clear example of this dichotomy; he
lived a very interesting and diverse life. He experienced every
worldly blessing early in his career and every spiritual blessing
after trusting in Christ. As he looked back on his journey, he
found that through every high and every low, it was not *what*
he had that brought contentment, but *who* he had.

It is our relationship with Christ, and the presence and
strength of His Holy Spirit, that enables us to overcome anything we face in this world. It is this truth that strengthens a
widow as she stands for hours at the casket, or the patient who

is on round twelve of chemotherapy. It is the assurance and contentment in Christ that enables a mother to get out of bed the day after her miscarriage or empowers the double amputee to continue to serve God and his family when his identity feels lost. This truth allows the husband to stand tall when the company lays him off, because his contentment is found in Christ and not in his profession.

I do not know what you are struggling with in your life or what challenges you to make it through the day. What I do know is that if your contentment is dependent upon anything other than Christ, then you will be a victim to your circumstances. If you listen to Paul, you will learn the secret of contentment, which is found only in Christ and will enable you to overcome.

Day 21

Fan the Flame

2 Timothy 1:3-9

> For this reason I remind you to kindle afresh the gift of God which is in you through the laying on of my hands. For God has not given us a spirit of timidity, but of power and love and discipline.
> —2 Timothy 1:6-7

Even though Timothy was called to be the pastor of Ephesus, he was still a relatively young believer and new to the office of overseer. In Paul's first letter to Timothy, we learn that this young leader would have to face many obstacles and false teachings in the church. It would be imperative for him to remember that God had not only called him, but also had equipped him to accomplish the mission at Ephesus. In 2 Timothy 1:3, we can see that Paul was praying for him, and we see in 2 Timothy 1:5 that Timothy had been taught sound doctrine and faith.

However, a key point to grasp is that it was up to Timothy to take ownership of the unique gift God had given him. He did not need to shrink away in fear; instead, Paul encouraged him to press on in boldness because of his love for God and the discipline of the Word of God. This need to take ownership of our specific gifts is not only true for Timothy, but for us as well.

There are habits that every believer needs to develop, and we have already talked about several of them. We need to be people of prayer, patience, and planning. We need to be steadfast and to persevere during the trials of life. Our foundation needs to be built upon Christ, and we need to be rooted in His Word. We are to be connected to a local body of believers for support and encouragement. We are to fan into flames the spiritual gift God gave us (2 Timothy 1:6).

Many people will say that they do not have a spiritual gift, but God tells us that all believers have been gifted by His grace. These gifts come in many different forms, but each gift originates from the same Spirit. Granted, they may be designed for different ministries, but each unique talent comes from the same God (1 Corinthians 12:4-5). Please, never doubt that you have been blessed with a spiritual gift to serve God.

It is important to understand that just because you are not as gifted in one area of ministry as someone else does not mean that you are exempt from service. No one who is a follower of Christ is exempt from serving Him. We are all commanded to proclaim the gospel and to *do the work of an evangelist* (2 Timothy 4:5). We are all commanded to be prayer warriors for other believers and for those who do not know Christ. We are all commanded to gather together to encourage, love, and correct one another.

However, you also have been given a gift according to God's grace for the purpose of glorifying God and supporting the body of Christ. Are you a musician or singer who could enhance worship for others? Are you comfortable talking to strangers? Perhaps you could greet visitors at the door on Sunday morning. Are you good at organizing events and schedules that could help with outreach or fellowship events? Are you a good steward with your money so that you could bring insight to the budget committee? Are you financially well-off and able to help fund a ministry or pay a child's way to camp? Are you a prayer warrior who could dedicate large amounts of your week to covering God's church in prayer? Are you retired? Maybe you have been given some of the most important gifts of availability and willingness. Take a moment to reflect and ask the Father to show you what gifts He desires for you to use daily.

Find out what your spiritual gift is and fan it into a glowing flame. Take a spiritual gifts questionnaire or ask another believer in your church to help you figure out how you can serve God if you do not know. Do not let the embers burn out.

Day 22

Do Not Get Distracted

2 Timothy 2:4; Joshua 1:7

No soldier in active service entangles himself in
the affairs of everyday life, so that he may please
the one who enlisted him as a soldier.
—2 Timothy 2:4

It is a daily challenge to remember that we are *fearfully and
wonderfully made* in the image of our God (Psalm 139:14). We
are all called to be missionaries for God's purpose and plan. We
have a mission to proclaim the good news of Jesus Christ and
to make disciples of all nations. Paul told Timothy that he did
not need to be entangled in the affairs of everyday life, but that
he (and we) should be like soldiers who listen to the orders of
their commanding officer; we are to listen to the voice of God.

As Joshua entered the promised land, God told him that
he had the difficult task of defeating the many enemies before
him. However, God admonished Joshua to not be afraid, for the
Almighty God was going to be with him. Even more than this,
God promised Joshua that he had already given the enemies
over to him. In short, God reminded Joshua that while his task
was important, he needed to remain focused. God commanded
him, *Do not turn from it to the right or to the left, so that you
may have success wherever you go* (Joshua 1:7). When Jesus sent
out the seventy in groups of two, He gave them instructions to
stay focused and not to take anything that would distract them
or to go anywhere that would hinder their progress. Likewise,
we must stay on mission.

The assignment that God has given His followers is too important for them to get distracted. Unfortunately, this world is full of distractions. Social media, streaming services, sports, and extracurricular activities demand our attention. You may stay up all night binge-watching the new Netflix series and never even glance at your Bible. You may spend all weekend with other children's parents at the ballfield, but never once approach the topic of Jesus or their salvation. We wonder if they would even listen to what you had to say after the horrible things you yelled at the referee. You are so focused on your new relationship that all your time and energy is poured into the new person in your life instead of into Christ.

The bills are piling up and your work is cutting hours, so your motivation is to stay afloat instead of deepening your walk with God. Husbands, wives, children, careers, money, sports, camping, hunting, sleeping, family time, church activities, vacations, concerts, cars, drinking, gambling, and your never-ending list of things to do around the house are just a few of the distractions we may face each day. There are some wonderful things on that list that need our attention, such as family and church, but not to the detriment of our relationship with God and spreading the gospel. God has called us to a heavenly mission with an eternal impact, and we cannot afford to be distracted.

Always Be Ready to Proclaim the Gospel

2 Timothy 4:1-8; 1 Peter 3:13-17

> But sanctify Christ as Lord in your hearts, always
> being ready to make a defense to everyone who
> asks you to give an account for the hope that is in
> you, yet with gentleness and reverence.
> —1 Peter 3:15

It is difficult to sit on the bench and watch the rest of your team play the game. Will you only get to play the last few minutes of a game when your efforts will have little or no impact on the results? Will the coach call your name at all? The lesson for us to learn is that every believer has a part to play in the expansion of the gospel. In other words, there is no bench-sitting when you belong to Christ. We are all "put in the game."

You may be the pastor of a megachurch or a faithful follower of Christ working in a factory, but you have a job to proclaim the gospel. Every player on the bench has spent time in the weight room, has practiced with teammates, and maybe even spent extra time improving his cardiovascular fitness. He is ready to go into the game when his name or number is called. The difference between this analogy and the Christian life is that while some players will sit on the bench their whole career, Christians are called to be ambassadors of Christ on a daily basis. We have to be ready to give a defense of our hope (1 Peter 3:15), who is Christ, and to preach the Word of God *in season and out of season* (2 Timothy 4:2).

How do we become ready to proclaim the gospel? We must

be rooted in God's Word in such a way that we not only know what it says, but we also understand what it means and know how to apply its message. This does not mean that we can just skim over a daily reading plan, trying to read the entire Bible in a year so that we can put a checkmark on our to-do list. Rather, it means that we must meditate on a passage of Scripture, learn the context, connect it to other Bible passages, and study the overall application for us today. We must pray over what we read and learn how to apply it.

There have been too many people who sit and listen to sermons and take every word the pastor speaks as truth. My prayer is that pastors are faithful to prepare and present a biblical message. However, the only way to know for sure that there is authority in what pastors say is to compare their message with God's Word. Second Timothy 2:15 says, *Be diligent to present yourself approved to God as a workman who does not need to be ashamed, accurately handling the word of truth.*

We must not only pray over what we are studying in God's Word, but we must also ask God for opportunities to pass on what we have learned to others. This may mean discipling young believers as they grow closer to Christ and deepen their faith. It could also mean explaining to an unbeliever truths that we have learned from God's Word. Perhaps our words could lead them to the point of conviction.

It is important for us to be praying for opportunities to proclaim the gospel, because the more we are praying for the lost, the more we will be looking for such opportunities. God is constantly opening doors of ministry for us, but many times we are not looking, not ready, or simply not motivated to share. I do not know about you, but I want to be ready because the coach has already called my name.

Do Not Be Surprised, but Rejoice!

1 Peter 4:12-17

Beloved, do not be surprised at the fiery ordeal
among you, which comes upon you for your testing, as though some strange thing were happening
to you; but to the degree that you share the sufferings of Christ, keep on rejoicing; so that also at
the revelation of His glory you may rejoice with
exultation.
—1 Peter 4:12-13

What a crazy thing to say – that we should rejoice in sufferings! Peter was writing this letter to the Christians who
were scattered throughout the region due to the persecution they
were facing because of their faith. He was basically telling them
to quit whining about their hardship because Christ endured so
much more. Jesus told His followers that the world hated Him,
and it would also hate those who follow Him (John 15:18-20).
This perverse and crooked world is broken by sin, and sadly,
the truth is that many unbelievers are against you. We should
not be surprised. We should rejoice in the fact that we share
everything with Christ, including His sufferings and His glory.

Yesterday you were encouraged to pray for opportunities to proclaim the gospel, but you must also be aware that
not every door that God opens leads to buried treasure. First
Corinthians 16:8-9 says, *But I will remain in Ephesus until
Pentecost; for a wide door for effective service has opened to
me, and there are many adversaries.* God opened a door for

evangelism and discipleship, but the road was covered with obstacles and opposition. Following Christ was not easy for the Corinthians, and the book of Ephesians informs us that Timothy also had the difficult task of wading through many of these issues.

Do not get discouraged when your ministry is difficult or when you do not think you are making a difference. Our job is to be ready, be obedient, and rejoice that God is using us. If there are many adversaries and trials, then rejoice, because it means you are doing something right.

Day 25

You Would Not Understand Even If I Told You

Habakkuk 1:1-5

Look among the nations! Observe! Be astonished!
Wonder! Because I am doing something in your
days – you would not believe if you were told.
—Habakkuk 1:5

God is working and moving even when we cannot see Him. He is fully aware of the situation we are in and the circumstances surrounding us. It would be easy for us to look around and see a world that seems to be getting worse rather than better, and choose to give up. After twenty-five days of praying, studying, and proclaiming the gospel, you would think that things would be different. The reality is that many times we will plant seeds and never see growth or a harvest; those results are in God's hands.

Habakkuk was struggling with what he saw when he looked at God's people. He saw violence, iniquity, wickedness, destruction, strife, and perverted justice all around him. He could not understand why God was allowing such sinful behavior to take place among His people and its leadership. I imagine that you may be feeling the same way after seeing what God can do in a week with a small group of sold-out believers, and now you are seeing hardly anything happening in a church of fifty to a hundred so-called followers of Christ.

Like Habakkuk, we ask, "God, what are You doing? Why are You letting this happen? When are You going to do something?" God's answer to Habakkuk was a very short and simple response to a very complicated and heartfelt question. He said, *You would not believe if you were told*. He then said that He was doing something so amazing, so mind-numbing, that when Habakkuk saw it happen, he would not even be able to comprehend what was going on.

This situation is similar for today's believers. We are so arrogant that we think we know exactly what needs to be done and how it should be done. So when we see what God is doing, we may still question it. How many times do we have the right intentions and the right heart without humility? We may think, "God, You need to do something, but please follow these carefully prayed-over and planned-out steps."

In Habakkuk's situation, God chose to use the Chaldeans to punish the people of Judah for their sin. This concept of discipline was completely absurd to Habakkuk, but how often do we get an answer from God that is entirely different from what we were expecting? It reminds me of a gentleman from

Oklahoma who began praying for God to use him. He had a successful pharmacy in his hometown, and he decided to go on a mission trip to Thailand with a local church. While he was on the trip, God burdened his heart for the hill tribes in northern Thailand. So when he got home, he sold his pharmacy and moved his entire family to Chiang Mai. God does not follow our plan; we are to follow His.

It is a wonderful thing that you are burdened by the brokenness of this world and by the failure of the church, but the best thing we can do is to trust God and be obedient. We are not going to know how, why, or when – but we know that He will, and that is good enough for me.

God, How Can You Be Silent?
This Is Not Who You Are

Habakkuk 1:13

Your eyes are too pure to approve evil, and You can
not look on wickedness with favor. Why do You
look with favor on those who deal treacherously?
Why are You silent when the wicked swallow up
those more righteous than they?
—Habakkuk 1:13

After Habakkuk received the news that God had chosen the
wicked Chaldeans to punish Judah, he had a moment of
spiritual crisis: "God, why are You using the wicked to punish
the righteous? How can You approve of the lifestyle and sins
of the Chaldeans? Where is the wrath of Your justice on the
evil Chaldeans?" Everything that Habakkuk knew about the
character of God was being questioned, and he cried out to
God for answers.

There may have been times in your life when you were
having a spiritual crisis of faith, and it felt as if God was silent.
Maybe you lost a grandparent who was your spiritual mentor,
or your spouse woke up one day and said she did not love you
anymore, or the doctor said that the cancer is back, and it is
now in stage 4. You cry out to God, "This is not who You are!
You are a loving God! You are a God who heals and restores,"
and there is just silence. You see people around you living in
sin. On the outside, it may look like their lives are wonderful

and blessed. It appears that everything comes easy for them, but you seem to struggle everyday with everything. You ask in frustration, "God, what are You doing? How is this fair?"

First, the reason why the evil people of this world are not experiencing God's wrath is because God is still holding back His wrath. There is a term called "common grace" that is used to describe God's indiscriminate kindness to all people, both believers and unbelievers, through the daily blessings of earthly life. The grace is different from God's saving grace that is reserved for those who have trusted Him as Lord and Savior. One day, those who have rejected Christ will face the wrath of God, and those who have trusted Christ will be sheltered by His wonderful saving grace. God was not giving special blessings to the Chaldeans, but He was simply using them to bring discipline to His children.

Second, God was not approving the sinful behavior of the Chaldeans. Habakkuk used several verses to describe their horrible behavior. In verse 13, he implied that God was looking down *with favor* on this wicked nation. We can sometimes feel that way about the things taking place in our world today. However, the truth is that the righteous and the unrighteous, the good and the evil, will exist together until the final judgment. Matthew 13 says that the tares and the wheat will be allowed to grow together, but the tares will be cast into the eternal fire, and the wheat will be gathered into the storehouse. Just because God allows something to exist is not a stamp of approval on sinful behavior, but rather is a testimony to His grace and patience.

Day 27

Watch and Wait – It Comes in God's Time

Habakkuk 2:1-3

I will stand on my guard post and station myself
on the rampart; and I will keep watch to see what
He will speak to me, and how I may reply when I
am reproved.
—Habakkuk 2:1

It is understood that when you are waiting for something to
happen, the best thing you can do is find a distraction. If you
are consumed with the possibility of what is going to happen,
how it is going to happen, and when it is going to happen, then
you will accomplish nothing and nothing will ever happen.
However, this was exactly the opposite of what Habakkuk did as
he stood on guard keeping watch and waiting for God to speak.

I love deer hunting. I find a nice location where the deer
are traveling through, and I set up my deer stand or blind. The
morning of opening day of deer season, I get up early, find my
place, and wait. My ears are alert and my eyes are scanning
back and forth as I watch and wait. I imagine that this was the
posture of Habakkuk as he stood on the wall of the city waiting
for an answer to his prayer – and God answered.

He commanded Habakkuk to write His answer down so
that it would be permanent, plain, and public. God wanted
everyone to know that His goal would be accomplished, but
it would happen in His time and in His way. He assured them
that the day was coming. The time has been appointed, but we
must wait. We are to keep our ears open and our eyes moving

because before you know it, the sun will come up and pierce through the darkness. There is a moment right before the light chases away the shadows that you imagine what is standing before you in the woods. Were the sounds of rustling leaves squirrels or a ten-point buck? Was the knocking noise the sound of branches bouncing in the wind or antlers in the brush? All will be revealed when the sun comes up. All prayers will be answered when the Son of God returns.

Day 28

The Righteous Walk by Faith

Habakkuk 2:4

Behold, as for the proud one, his soul is not right within him; but the righteous will live by his faith.
—Habakkuk 2:4

In the middle of the book of Habakkuk we find a declaration that *the righteous will live by his faith.* This verse is quoted several times in the New Testament (Romans 1:17; Hebrews 10:38; Galatians 3:11) to help us understand the fullness of its meaning. It is also the verse that Martin Luther read that many scholars think may have started the Reformation.

For Habakkuk, this verse was a warning against pride and a charge to trust God above all else. Some people live by their achievements, their commitments, their feelings, or their circumstances. They trust that these things will bring about salvation, but they will find that their soul is not right with God. There are those who take pride in what they have and in what they can do. They take pride in their place in society, their intelligence, and even their religion. However, the only way to be found righteous before God is to live by faith and to trust fully and only in Him.

Every day we must make the conscious choice to live by faith and dependence on God instead of by pride and self-reliance. We must accept God's timing, guidance, and discipline even when we do not understand. Let us remember what God said: *For My thoughts are not your thoughts, nor are your ways My ways. . . . As the heavens are higher than the earth, so are My ways higher than your ways and My thoughts than your thoughts* (Isaiah 55:8-9).

There are several things that we will never be able to comprehend. The intricate details and inner workings of God and His character will confound us until He comes again. There are truths scattered throughout His written Word that will only be fully understood on the glorious day of His return. It is not meant for us to know everything, and we are incapable of retaining the infinite amount of knowledge that God possesses. The purpose of faith is not to attain knowledge; rather, it is to gain obedience. *The secret things belong to the LORD our God, but the things revealed belong to us and to our sons forever, that we may observe all the words of this law* (Deuteronomy 29:29).

God will not reveal every detail of His plan, but He will reveal enough for us to trust and obey. Let us cast aside our pride and walk by faith!

Day 29

The Lord Is God Alone;
There Is No One Like Him

Habakkuk 2:18-20

What profit is the idol when its maker has carved it, or an image, a teacher of falsehood? For its maker trusts in his own handiwork when he fashions speechless idols. Woe to him who says to a piece of wood, "Awake!" To a mute stone, "Arise!" And that is your teacher? Behold, it is overlaid with gold and silver, and there is no breath at all inside it. But the LORD is in His holy temple. Let all the earth be silent before Him.
—Habakkuk 2:18-20

As we come to the last two days of our journey together, I want to leave you with a truth that Habakkuk was reminded of as he was striving to walk by faith: *You are great, O Lord GOD; for there is none like You, and there is no God besides You* (2 Samuel 7:22). This proclamation was made throughout the Old Testament by Jeremiah, Samuel, Moses, and David. In all their experiences, there was nothing that compared to the holiness, power, and glory of God.

Habakkuk emphasized the meaningless act of placing our faith in man-made idols that cannot breathe, move, or speak. These idols are created; therefore, they can be destroyed. It is foolish to think that they hold any power. We might think it is strange that people would worship an inanimate object and call it a god, but is it any different than the idols we have created in our own lives? We may not have fashioned our idols out of wood, but our hearts are filled with the desire for wealth, possessions, advancement in our career, or our obsession with our children. We allow these things and many others to sit on the throne of our hearts as idols, and they can neither breathe, move, or speak – yet we give them our worship.

If we are going to be able to continue to live lives that are pleasing to God in the face of an apathetic church and a lost and dying world, then we need to remember that there is only one God and Savior Jesus Christ. When we are challenged, we are to turn to God's Word for wisdom and listen to His Spirit for guidance. Only God is omnipotent, omniscient, and omnipresent. Only God is holy, just, and good. Only Jesus is the perfect, acceptable sacrifice for the atonement of all sin. He is the one we serve. He is the only one we are to obey, and the only one worthy of our worship.

Habakkuk realized that both the righteous and the wicked would stand before the one true, holy God, and their response would be the same: silence. My prayer is that when that day comes, my life will have been one that was poured out as a living sacrifice, acceptable to God, and not a life consumed by idols. Please reflect on this question: "What will your life be?"

Day 30

Be Patient; Justice Is on the Way

Habakkuk 3:16-19

Yet I will exult in the LORD, I will rejoice in the
God of my salvation. The Lord GOD is my strength,
and He has made my feet like hinds' feet, and
makes me walk on my high places.
—Habakkuk 3:18-19

Habakkuk soon found himself having a completely different
perspective than he did in chapter one. He looked around
and saw the failures of Judah and the wickedness of the surrounding nations. He questioned God's compassion and choice
of discipline. He questioned God's grace toward the wicked and
the timing of His judgments.

However, by the third chapter of the book of Habakkuk,
he was patiently waiting for the Lord to bring down His judgment upon Judah by way of the Chaldeans. The promised land
of God's people was filled with barren fields and empty stalls.
The wine vats were bare and the trees were no longer bloom-
ing. Habakkuk knew that this current judgment was only for a
season, and he rejoiced, even when he did not know how long
it would last or when reprieve would come.

This is the change of heart that needs to occur with us today.
We need to learn to look at our situation through the lens of
God's Word and have a change of perspective. Remember that
God is in control and that no wickedness will go unpunished.
Justice is on the way. It will arrive in God's time and according

to His purpose. We can rejoice to know that the faithful will receive their reward and the wicked will receive their judgment.

It is our responsibility to proclaim the gospel and help as many people as we can to cross over from spiritual death to life in Christ. Let us be the watchmen (and women) who sound the warning of the approaching destruction. As God's children, we acknowledge and appreciate the reality of the second coming of Christ. We know that Christ will separate the goats from the sheep, the tares from the wheat, and the bad fish from the good. The certainty that everyone will stand before the great white throne, and the fact that we hold the hope of salvation in Jesus Christ, should empower us to be bold in our witness. Yes, we are waiting for Christ to come and receive His bride unto Himself and to judge those who have rejected Him, but we are not to wait passively. We are to be active and joyful and exalt Christ as we share the good news to everyone who will listen. Repent. Justice is on the way.

Epilogue

It is amazing what God can do with very little. Jesus took five barley loaves and two fish and fed more than five thousand people (John 6). God commanded Gideon to take three hundred men armed with nothing but trumpets, pitchers, and torches to surround the Midianites and the Amalekites in battle. God caused confusion, the two enemy armies destroyed themselves, and Israel was victorious (Judges 7). Elisha met a widow who was afraid that her two sons would become slaves if she could not pay her debt. The only thing of value she owned was a single jar of oil. Elisha commanded her to borrow all the empty jars she could, and God multiplied her oil until every vessel was overflowing (2 Kings 4).

This is not a new attribute of God, but an eternal one. It is a truth that was present in the first verses of God's Word: *In the beginning God created the heavens and the earth. The earth was formless and void, and darkness was over the surface of the deep; and the Spirit of God was moving over the surface of the waters. Then God said, "Let there be light"; and there was light* (Genesis 1:1-3). The earth was *formless and void*; in other words, it was nonexistent. There was nothing physically present for God to work with, yet in His sovereignty and omnipotence, He was able to create all that we know. What an amazing God we serve!

Since we know that God can do miraculous things with absolutely nothing, it should not surprise us that He can accomplish many wonderful things through you and me. Philippians 1:6 says, *For I am confident of this very thing, that He who began a good work in you will perfect it until the day of Christ Jesus.* Paul reminds us in the next chapter that *it is God who is at work in you, both to will and to work for His good pleasure* (Philippians 2:13). The challenge is not in God's ability, but in our willingness. It is my prayer that you realize that God has used you in some mighty ways over the last couple of months as you were obedient.

I know that it is difficult to take time away from work and family for a weeklong mission trip every year, but let me give you one last challenge. Give God 2 percent of your time! Give God 2 percent of your time and watch how He will transform the other 98 percent. There are 365 days in a year, and 2 percent is seven days, or one week. There are 1,440 minutes in a day, and 2 percent is about twenty-nine minutes. There are 168 hours in a week, and 2 percent is three and a half hours.

Imagine what would happen if you went on one mission trip every year, spent thirty minutes a day in God's Word, and spent three and a half hours every week serving others. Two percent does not seem like a lot. What did I really accomplish for the kingdom of God in one week? The answer is: "More than you will ever know."

I pray that you have grown over the last couple of months and that you saw God do some amazing things on your trip, but He is not done with you yet. Whatever you have to offer, no matter how small you think it might be, give it to God and see what incredible things He will do.

Lee Davis is a pastor in Kentucky who has served in ministry for more than twenty years. He loves to travel all over the world proclaiming the good news of Jesus Christ and making disciples. If he is not on a mission trip or serving his church, then Lee is encouraging other local pastors and believers.

www.ladministries.com